Praise for *The*

"If you've ever wondered what sha
tice of this venerable tradition blesses our lives and
if you live and work within a shamanic worldview and need a boost—
then consider yourself fortunate to have Colleen's passionate voice and
compassionate nature as 'one who knows' through *The Hollow Bone*.
Colleen has done a masterful job in showing how shamanism fits into
our world today, why it is important, and how to find your own way
in making this world a better place for all. Read this book as soon as
you can—and 'see the soul of the world in every rock, stream, bird,
and cloud.'"

—Nan Moss and David Corbin,
authors of *Weather Shamanism:
Harmonizing Our Connection with the Elements*

"This guide to spiritual knowledge and wisdom empowers the reader
to find their spiritual path and the connection of all life—animate and
inanimate, visible and invisible. Colleen shines a light on ancient ways
while helping you to integrate tools and spirituality into daily life to
elicit powerful personal and global transformation. A must read for a
beginner on the path!"

—Margaret Ann Lembo, author of *Chakra Awakening:
Transform Your Reality Using Crystals, Color,
Aromatherapy and the Power of Positive Thought*

"A fascinating look at a worldview that is both ancient and timeless. Like any shamanic practice worth its salt, reading *The Hollow Bone*
will challenge cherished beliefs and stretch readers way beyond comfort. Open it, read it, and apply it—only if you dare."

—Mark Stavish, author of *Between the Gates: Lucid Dreaming,
Astral Projection, and the Body of Light in Western Esotericism*

"A comprehensive and scholarly book on shamanism that will bring this ancient and powerful spiritual practice into the contemporary world at a time when it is most needed."

—Steven Farmer, PhD, author of
Earth Magic and *Animal Spirit Guides*

"A must read for anyone interested in shamanic life and practice. This book delivers the vital message that shamanism is both heart-centered and earth-honoring and shamanic healers are 'hollow bones' of the Spirit. I am putting it at the top of my students' book list."

—C. Michael Smith (Mikkal), author of
Jung and Shamanism in Dialogue

"A comprehensive exploration of shamanism and its modern application, *The Hollow Bone* brings clarity to a word often misused and misunderstood. True to Colleen Deatman's expressed purpose, her words are a bridge between the worlds and bring the possibility of Spirit to the collective challenges we all face. Over the years, I have hoped for a book that demystifies shamanic work and makes it accessible to a wider audience. This is that book."

—Myron Eshowsky, shamanic mediator/trauma
healing activist, and author of *Peace with Cancer:
Shamanism as a Spiritual Approach to Healing*;

The
Hollow Bone

A Field Guide
to Shamanism

COLLEEN DEATSMAN

WEISERBOOKS
San Francisco, CA / Newburyport, MA

First published in 2011 by Weiser Books, an imprint of
Red Wheel/Weiser, LLC
With offices at:
665 Third Street, Suite 400
San Francisco, CA 94107
www.redwheelweiser.com

Barton, Barb. "Circles," © 1993, *From the Eye of Hawk* album. Reproduced with
permission. *www.barbbarton.com*

Nepo, Mark. "What Sustains." From his forthcoming book, *Reduced to Joy*. Reproduced with the author's permission.

Bailey-Lessirard, Michele. "She Knew." From the author's blog, New Moon
Journal. Reproduced with permission. *www.newmoonjournal.blogs.com/*
the_new_moon_journal/220_chironthe_bridge_builder

ISBN: 978-1-57863-498-9

Library of Congress Cataloging-in-Publication Data

Deatsman, Colleen, 1960-
 The hollow bone : a field guide to shamanism / Colleen Deatsman.
  p. cm.
 Includes bibliographical references and index.
 ISBN 978-1-57863-498-9 (alk. paper)
 1. Shamanism. I. Title.
 BF1611.D326 2011
 201'.44--dc23
                           2011023354

Cover design by Jim Warner
Interior layout by Jane Hagaman
Typeset in Adobe Garamond Pro

Printed in Canada
TCP
10 9 8 7 6 5 4 3 2 1

The paper used in this publication meets the minimum requirements of the American National Standard for Information Sciences—Permanence of Paper for Printed
Library Materials Z39.48-1992 (R1997).

To Pat

My beloved husband and life partner, on all levels, in all things. With you by my side, my love, I am able to be the best me that I can be. I am truly blessed and deeply grateful to share this journey of life with such an impeccable man and beautiful soul. Thank you for your deep, unwavering love and rock-steady light. You have a unique and special way of helping me stay connected with the Earth while I am exploring the Cosmos and beyond, and that helps me fully open to Spirit flow, so beautiful living and healing books like this can happen.

Contents

Part Four
Shamanism and Healing

Part Five
Personal Healing, Shamanism, and Being of Service
Your Calling

Foreword

A way of life is dissolving right before our eyes, and everywhere people are looking for inspiration. We need to know that there are solutions to the challenges we are facing, including finding new livelihoods as our careers evaporate before our eyes; stemming a climate crisis that is already wreaking profound havoc; raising children to be able to handle a future filled with uncertainties; finding uncontaminated, healthful foods to eat; and caring for a generation of elders whose bodies are outliving their spirits.

We need to learn how to be the new dreamers and how to weave into being a new way of life that is filled with love, light, harmony, peace, health, joy, and equality for every living thing. Shamanism is the oldest spiritual practice known to humankind. Many anthropologists have dated the practice back over 100,000 years, and it was and is practiced in every culture the world over. It is a spirituality based on healing and living in balance with each other and the natural world, and it survives in its many forms because it has been so successful at helping people and communities heal and stay whole.

Think about it. I'll bet one of your ancestors practiced shamanism.

Yes, it is remarkable that shamanism has survived so many thousands of years. It is also remarkable that there is such a resurgence of interest in it in the Western world today—remarkable, but not really all that mysterious.

As Colleen Deatsman makes so clear in her introduction to shamanism, *The Hollow Bone, A Field Guide to Shamanism,* shamans are and always have been the doctors and psychotherapists of their communities. We need our healers. Traditionally, the health of individuals and communities was the responsibility of the shamans. If the shamans did not do their jobs well, people starved, people died needlessly. Today, at this time of great change and upheaval, when we are being called to transform and act on behalf of all of life, we need our healers in a big way, and shamanism has much to teach us.

Shamans believe that the illnesses and the problems we are facing today stem from a disharmonious way of life. Shamanism teaches us that we are connected to a web of life and that every change we make ripples throughout the entire web of life. What we do makes a difference. *Everything* we do makes a difference. By teaching us that no effort, no matter how small, is in vain, shamanism offers optimism in these otherwise dark times.

Shamanism is a spiritual practice that is based on divine revelation, which means that we all can access spiritual knowledge to guide us in our lives and the times ahead. Shamanic practice requires no outside authorities, intermediaries, or even beliefs. Instead, shamanism provides a series of accessible tools that put you in contact with your deep inner knowing and spiritual allies that can provide insight and healing. Most importantly, shamanism is a way of life.

There is a great deal of freedom in working with shamanism, as there is no one set way of doing things; we are all required to find our own way on the path. There are guidelines that can help us, and at the same time, we can receive our own personal revelations that keep the work fresh and inspired.

What Colleen Deatsman does so successfully throughout this book is outline exactly how the practice of shamanism can assist in our personal healing and the healing of the planet. She illumines us as she gives us an overview of what shamanism is. Without being technical, she takes us into the world and the work of the shaman, showing us how shamanism has evolved and how it is as powerful a way to work and heal in the twenty-first century as it was for the first humans thousands and thousands of years ago. She brilliantly describes how the shamanic way of life can bring us back into harmony with each other and the planet and how it enables healing and

The Hollow Bone

evolution to higher states of consciousness—for us as individuals, as communities, and as a planet.

At one time, Colleen was my student, and it has been a great pleasure to see her develop into such an outstanding shamanic practitioner and esteemed colleague. Colleen teaches and writes from her own experience of using shamanic practices to heal herself, and her writing and teaching have added greatly to the field of contemporary shamanism.

I am grateful to Colleen for writing *The Hollow Bone, A Field Guide to Shamanism*. It does a wonderful job of demystifying the ancient practice of shamanism and showing even our skeptical friends how shamanism can be used today to empower all of us during these times of change.

Together we can weather the current chaos. The 100,000-year-old practices of shamanism point the way ahead. Read on, learn more about this ancient way of life, and be inspired!

Sandra Ingerman, author of
Soul Retrieval and
Shamanic Journeying: A Beginner's Guide

Acknowledgments

Special thanks and immense gratitude to:

Durrette, for being my sweet soul sister. What a powerful journey we have been on together for years and lifetimes. This book wouldn't be what it is without your special touch! I am indebted to you for your editing expertise, sharp eagle eye, and precious, steadfast, loving friendship! Thank you for the semicolons, our soul connection and love, and everything!

Jason, for being a true, dear friend and soul brother through thick and thin, life and death, and for saving my life, on and off the computer. How do I get to be so lucky as to come back lifetime after lifetime to be soul-connected with you? Here's to lessons learned, friends lost and kept, and realizing what matters most in life! Thank you for converting the pictures in this book into beautiful high-resolution tifs. You saved me once again and helped many see clearly the beauty in shamanism.

Lauren, not only for being my beautiful daughter, but for also being a dear and fun friend. Your wonderful company and delicious, healthy meals over the course of this book-writing journey have been delightful gifts that I will treasure forever. Thank you for your love, support, and encouragement!

LaVon and Donna Deatsman, for being such supportive parents, for your unconditional love, and for teaching me so much about life, love, Nature, and what really matters.

Laura and Erin, for your love, understanding, and support of my dreams, endeavors, and need to dance to the beat of a different drum. It really means a lot that you see me for me; know that I see you for you!

The Helping Spirits and Ancestors, who orchestrated, guided, shared, and wrote this extraordinary journey.

Caroline Pincus, associate publisher, Red Wheel/Weiser Books and Conari Press, whose vision made this book a reality. I love working with you and Red Wheel/Weiser! Thank you so much for your brilliant guidance! I especially thank you for your patience as I figured out what a high-resolution tif was and found my go-to man to get it done.

Amy Rost, editor, for your careful, compassionate, honest, hands-on work. It's a blessing to work with you. Your thoughtful, thorough, and skilled approach not only carefully preserved the voice and information, but it also gave this book the clear flow that will help readers enjoy, soak in, and understand the contents. Hats off to you!

Dennis Fitzgerald, production director, and Susie Pitzen, assistant production editor, Red Wheel/Weiser, for your time, energy, expertise, and diligence to make this book look great!

Special thanks to my beloved, dedicated Circle Family: Carlton, Durrette, Mark, Mary, Laura G., Robbyn, Laura M., Marisa, Amanda, Miriam, Jen, Lori, Signe, Sue, Jason, Daniel, Tina, Jan Sc., Dan, Jan Sh., Brenda, John B., Erin., Charley, Geta, James, Mary Lou, Seth, Jesse, Charles, Shina, Kitty, Paul H., Debbie, Shauna, Karen Ow., Lisa H., Linda K., Linda H., Brad, Jean, Joy, Jane, Karen C., Karen O., Sabrina, Michael S., Pam, Tammy, Kate, Lucy H., Paula, Sarah, Joe, Arlene, Renee, Jan Sa., Amy, Joan, Jami, Curt, Melissa, Katherine, Jennifer, Marcy, Shirley, Nancy, Lisa F., Gin, Anya, Linda Mc., Samantha, Laura R., Martha, and Pat. You beautiful people are the heart and soul of shamanism.

My phenomenal life, circle, and shamanic friends—fellow journeyers who honor the "Spirit-that-moves-in-themselves-and-all-things" (readers, question-askers, seekers, finders, clients, healers, participants, students, apprentices, assistants, peers, colleagues, and teachers). We are all participants, teachers, and stewards of circles, within circles, within circles, in our own ways, throughout time and space. It is so, and I am deeply grateful for you.

Judy, for being my dearly beloved wise-woman mentor, colleague, and soul-comrade.

Barb Barton, for shining so radiantly in my life and the world. Bears and Moose belong in the Woods together.

Sincere gratitude to Thomas Banyacya Jr., Theresa Odette Siedner, Bill Sanda, Nana Vimla Eufemia Cholac Chicol, Dr. Larry Peters, Joy Markgraf, Martha and Todd Lucier, Shamanism Canada, Marco Nuñez Zamolloa, Angaangaq Angakkorsuaq, Ice Wisdom, Don Esteban Tamayo, Mama Rosita Tamayo, Esteban Tamayo Jr., Daniel Koupermann, Barb Barton, Michele Grace Bailey-Lessirard, Mark Nepo, Deanna Slate, Shilo Satran, Manataka American Indian Council, Smoke Signals Newsletter, Gijsbert (Nick) van Frankenhuyzen, Robbyn Smith, Hazel Ridge Farm, Sleeping Bear Press, Gretchen Crilly McKay, Adam Kane, Sacred Circle New Age, Brian Corbiere, Bibamikowi Studios, Bartholamew Dean, Tim and Candy Strain, Illyana Balde, Marisol Villanueva, the International Council of Thirteen Indigenous Grandmothers, World Pulse, Nan Moss, David Corbin, and Sandra Ingerman—for your generosity in sharing your beautiful, Spirit-gifted artwork, photographs, quotes, songs, poems, and stories in this book.

My humble, compassionate, Spirit-connected teachers—Sandra Ingerman, Tom Cowan, Dr. Larry Peters, Myron Eshowsky, Dr. Michael Harner, Nan Moss, David Corbin, Patrick Jasper Lee, and Judy—for living shamanism and sharing it with the world. I bow to you in deep respect.

Introduction

Today a new sun rises for me; everything lives, everything is animated, everything seems to speak to me of my passion, everything invites me to cherish it.

Ninon de l'Enclos, french author (1620–1705)

I am deeply honored to author this introductory book on shamanism, a way of healing, being, and living that is near and dear to my heart and soul.

I grew up in a small, rural town in central Michigan, where we spent nearly every waking moment outdoors. I learned how to play, swim, climb trees, camp, fish, hunt, wander the fields and forests, talk to the animals, and know Nature and Spirit as cherished friends. My dreams have always been filled with visions, and my desire to live in close connection with the Earth and Spirit has kept me exploring the messages of those dreams and the beauty and wonder of Nature. During my adolescent years, I devoured every book I could get my hands on about Native Americans, indigenous peoples of differing ethnicities, and mountain men. I longed to live as they did and many still do, honoring the Waters, enveloped by the Land and Sky, in balance with the Elements, listening to the omens, talking with the Weather Spirits.

As I became an adult, wife, mother of three, and weekend-warrior athlete with a full-time counseling career, my endeavors distracted me from this journey. My focus, time, and energies were caught up in daily living and excelling in all that I did. These stresses created an imbalance in my soul, energy field, and connection with Spirit, though I didn't recognize this imbalance until years later, when chronic fatigue immune dysfunction syndrome (CFIDS), fibromyalgia, and a slew of other physical breakdowns began to take a caustic toll. That was in the 1980s, a time when the medical community didn't understand what was happening to people presenting with symptoms of these conditions. Because doctors couldn't even diagnose the conditions, they certainly couldn't offer sound treatment or potential cures.

The numerous and mysterious chronic symptoms continued to worsen, deteriorating my body and eating away at my life. Finally, in the mid-1990s, I was diagnosed with Epstein-Barr and cytomegalo viruses, two of the purported causes of CFIDS and fibromyalgia. When I was advised to go home and rest, since there was no known medical treatment, I went nuts inside!

I refused to live my life as a victim of this illness. The warrior in me came alive, and I began looking for healing alternatives. I tried everything I could find in an attempt to heal. I took every herb and supplement that claimed to boost the immune system. I received massage, acupuncture, chiropractic, and energy bodywork, to name a few. All of these things helped keep me functioning, but they did not cure the beastly illness.

Something was missing—something deeper.

As soon as I realized this, a door opened. Stephanie and Kate, fellow coworkers at Community Mental Health and founders of Spirit Weavers, an organization devoted to providing shamanic healing and training, were hosting a weekend workshop called "Basic Shamanism," taught by Myron Eshowsky, through the Foundation for Shamanic Studies. I felt a powerful compulsion to attend. I couldn't shake the inner knowing that this workshop would lead me to the life I had so desperately craved for so very long.

During my first shamanic journey (or trance), I was very still and patient, something I had not been in ordinary reality. I felt at home and connected—also something I did not feel in ordinary reality. For the first time in many years, I was in a place where I belonged. I felt the Earth's protection and nurturance.

As part of my journey, I was sitting quietly by a mountain lake when my Power Animal (a Helping Spirit in animal form) stepped out of the willows along the edge and began to speak with me. He described in detail the ways I was wandering away from my soul destiny and participating in activities that were distracting me from what I needed to be doing. He shared that my physical challenges were caused by separation from Spirit and my soul-self and by energy mismanagement; the illness was my wake-up call, an opportunity to heal myself and refocus my life on the work of my soul.

I was amazed, but I knew all that he said was true. I expressed my regrets and my desire to reconnect with him and my soul purpose. He asked me to honor him and myself by doing less and spending more time just being. He encouraged me to spend time in his environment (Spirit world), to drum and journey daily, and to walk the path of awareness and connectedness in my everyday life. Then, we just were, being together, sharing, exchanging, and blending energy and essence, which materialized as waves of vibrant color. He showed me how, by being still and aware, I could *be*.

Within moments, the personal experience of my journey expanded to include the whole workshop room, where it seemed that rather than one drummer, there were many Spirit shamans, drumming their healing and sharing their power. From within my journey, I felt the whole room vibrating with the energy of the drums and the Spirits. The energy created by the steady rhythm then intensified as the songs and calls of what seemed like hundreds of birds added to the power. I felt the drumming and the bird songs inside of me, vibrating my heart and opening my soul. My heart ached from expansion, so much so that I actually rubbed the area on my physical body. I felt myself crack open down the middle. I let out the pain I had been holding and let in the vibrant colors.

I was reluctant to return with the callback signal. I had found my home. I had found my healing power. I had found my soul. I found my connection to the All.

What I didn't know then was that I had also found my soul's purpose: to bridge the worlds and bring Spirit energies into action for myself, others, and ultimately the world.

The first peace, which is the most important, is that which comes within the souls of people when they realize their relationship, their oneness with the universe and all its powers, and when they realize that at the center of the universe dwells the Great Spirit, and that this center is really everywhere, it is within each of us.
—Black Elk, *The Sacred Pipe*

My story shows but one example of the many ways that Spirit makes our calling known to us. Unbeknownst to me then, it was also a classic wounded-healer story. But there was much more to it than just the healing and the calling I received. It was a call to action and to an awareness of the Spirit that moves in all things, all the time—all day and night, 24/7/365—in everyday living.

The soul and Spirit work that my Power Animal talked with me about in that first journey, and on many subsequent journeys, led me to discover many beautiful gifts—gifts I would then use for healing, for living in balance and wholeness, and for being of service to others.

Like most shamans and shamanic practitioners, I never intended or wanted to be a healer, shamanic practitioner, teacher, or even an author. I wanted to be a biologist of one flavor or another. I wanted to be outdoors, immersed in Nature, exploring and helping to save the precious and beautiful gifts of Mother Earth that so many people take for granted. Mostly, I wanted to preserve the forests, explore the oceans as a steward of Jacques Cousteau's *Calypso,* and save the whales. I joined Greenpeace, honed my endurance-swimming aptitude, and pictured myself hanging from a whaling ship in a wet suit with "Save me!" painted on it in bold red letters. Apparently Spirit and my soul had a different plan for whom I would serve and how.

Now I am in service through shamanic healing, teaching, and writing, and I'm loving every single moment of it because shamanism is my soul's purpose and passion. I am also in service by being an aware and engaged wife and mom, neighbor and friend. It is a blessing to help people awaken, shift consciousness, ease pain and suffering, eliminate illness, connect with Spirit, and find the power and strength that lives within them. In a way, helping people in these ways saves souls, and perhaps the ripple effect will also help to save the whales, the oceans, the forests, the Earth, Nature, our planet, the universe, and beyond.

No, *I* am not saving your soul. *You* are the one who saves your soul. Shamans—shamanic practitioners, teachers, and writers—merely provide signs, messages, guideposts, bleeps of light, energetic jump starts. Working in unison with your soul, shamans hang from the vessel of Spirit, wearing a wet suit with "Save me!" painted on it for your eyes, your heart, your mind, and your inner knowing to see, if you choose.

In my fourth book, *Seeing in the Dark*, I wrote:

> The shamanic path is the path of the heart and the soul. It is a path of beauty, wholeness, sacred living, oneness and connectedness with all things and non-things, awareness, mindfulness, respect, honor, and gratitude. It's a path of extraordinary moments when Nature and Spirit speak more clearly than the racket of our mental chatter and we stop everything for that moment and take notice, listening and feeling the message. It is a path where the central focus of life is creating balance, harmony, impeccability, and wholeness. It is a path that requires integrity and honesty—with one's self and others. The shamanic path is a loving, healing path that invites all, while being a truth-revealing path, turning away initiates not yet ready to face the awesome truth of reality. For those who will continually accept the challenge, typically a daily choice, I invite you into the sacred circle of personal shamanic practitioners; a circle where healing, growth, change and transformation are constants and miracles happen.

The purpose of this, my fifth book is to share this way of living beyond the ordinary, which we call shamanism. This is a what-is-shamanism book, rather than a how-to-practice-shamanism book. It illuminates what is often considered to be a mysterious path and answers many frequently asked questions, such as: What is shamanism? What are the beliefs and understandings inherent to shamanism? Who are the shamans? What do shamans do? How does one become a shaman? Can anyone be a shaman, and if I am interested in becoming one, where can I learn more?

I hope you enjoy the journey.

Note to the reader: You will likely notice a shift in format of capitalizations between the introduction and main text of this book. The capitalization within the introduction, my personal account, represents my personal beliefs and perceptions that all things are living, are souls, and are to be honored and respected as such; therefore, in my view, the terms for these things would be capitalized. But capitalizing terms for so many things that most view as mundane and inanimate could be distracting to the reader, so the rest of the text will follow the usual rules of grammar. Please know that in my view, in my heart and soul, all beings mentioned and described in this text are honored and sacred, regardless of whether or not the words naming them are capitalized.

Part One

Shamanism and the Shamanic Worldview

Chapter 1

The Spirituality of the Ages

Shamanism is many things to many people—at its core it is an ancient spiritual tradition dedicated to becoming fully human. Through partnership with the compassionate spirits, shamanic practitioners bring blessings of balance and healing to our world.

Nan Moss and David Corbin,
Weather Shamanism

Shamanism is the path of immediate and direct personal contact with Spirit, deeply intuitive, and not subject to definition, censorship, or judgment by others.

Hank Wesselman and Sandra Ingerman,
Awakening to the Spirit World

Though shamanism is the oldest living path of spirituality and healing, many people have never heard of it or don't know what it is. "Shamanism is the most ancient spiritual practice known to mankind and is the 'ancestor' of all our modern religions," Hank Wesselman and Sandra Ingerman say in *Awakening to the Spirit World*.

"As a method, it is a form of meditation combined with focused intention to accomplish various things."[1] The term *shamanism* refers to actions and movements made based on spirit connections; those actions and movements vary according to the culture, community, discipline, purpose, training, calling, beliefs, and interpretations of the shamanic practitioners, as well as the spirit guidance and clients involved. Shamanism is spirit in action in living and healing for oneself, others, and the world.

As Nan Moss and David Corbin's quote explains, shamanism is many things to many people. It is a way of life and a practice that is rich in tradition, eclecticism, and mysticism. In the world today, there is confusion about what shamanism is and who the shamans are; the confusion exists not only in science and everyday vernacular and thought, but also among indigenous peoples, shamanic groups, and practitioners. Another word for confusion is *mystification,* and since shamanism is steeped in mystery, confusion about it is not surprising.

Shamanism is a path of direct revelation that is not subject to definition, censorship, or judgment by others, as Ingerman and Wesselman make clear in their quote at the very beginning of the chapter. Additionally, shamanism is personal, idiosyncratic, cross-cultural, and not owned by any person or peoples. The earth is shared by all people, yet individuals experience the earth in their own ways. Similarly, shamanism is shared by people around the world, yet each person experiences shamanism in his or her own way.

Shamanism is not a religion, nor does it have a doctrine, dogma, holy book, or set of rules to adhere to. Shamanism embodies the most widespread and time-tested practical system of spirituality and mind-body-soul healing known to humankind. It encompasses a timeless wisdom of indigenous cultures shared around the globe and passed down through tens of thousands of years to us, the recipient descendants.

Shamanism is not a religion, but the most widespread and time-tested practical system of spirituality and mind-body-soul healing known to humankind.

According to some reports supported by various archeological and anthropological discoveries, shamanism is estimated to have been an effective

The Hollow Bone

set of beliefs, actions, and healing methods for well over 50,000 years. In 1972, French archeologists working at the Hortus site in southern France unearthed a 50,000-year-old Neanderthal burial site. They found the body of a man wearing a leopard hide. The claws and tail of the hide were still intact, but there were no leopard bones in the grave. Most scientists accept that the Neanderthal man found at the Hortus site was a shaman. Archeological and anthropological records show us that tribal shamans in many cultures have worn the heads, furs, and other body parts of animals during ritual and healing ceremonies. The shamans are commonly buried with these and other ceremonial tools.

Shamanism is estimated to have been an effective set of beliefs, actions, and healing methods for well over 50,000 years—since before people were even people.

Pictographs and petroglyphs bearing shamanic images of people wearing animal and bird masks, dancing ecstatically or sitting in trance states, and interacting with images thought to represent a power or energy emitted from animals and

Figure 1

other unknown beings exist in multitudes of locations around the world. Newspaper Rock, shown in Figure 1, rises above the road and river on the way to the southern entrance of Canyonlands National Park in southern Utah. The rock contains a petroglyph, a carving in the sandstone, that clearly depicts over 2,000 years of life activity in the Fremont, Anasazi, Navajo, and Anglo cultures. It is one example of thousands of rock carvings and paintings from around the world that give us insight into shamans of the past.

Figure 2

Archeology, anthropology, and ancient artwork, as well as other evidence, point to the fact that shamanism has been around since before people were even people. It outlived the Neanderthal and has flourished for tens of thousands of years to the present day. Perhaps even more important to the human psyche and soul, every culture on the planet is rich in stories, myths, legends, and

If shamanism can endure 50,000 years of change, it can help us during these times of change.

teachings passed down in oral traditions, speaking to the longevity of shamanism as a way of life and healing.

Perhaps shamanism has survived the ages because it is experiential, practical, interactive, creative, and can be altered based on direct revelation and what is needed in each unique set of circumstances. Certainly, if shamanism can endure through all the changes of well over 50,000 years, and even the death of an entire species, it can help us during these times of change.

Those Who See in the Dark

Who are these extraordinary people who imitated the sounds of animals in the dark, or drank tobacco juice through funnels, or wore collars filled with stinging ants? —Jeremy Narby and Francis Huxley, *Shamans Through Time*

A practitioner of shamanism is known as a shaman.

Figure 2 gives us a glimpse of just one culture's extraordinary shamans. Haru (left), leader and peacemaker of his people, and his father, Univu (right), medicine man, pictured in ceremonial prayer, are from Amazonia Brazil, the place of the rainforest (the land of the big trees). This photograph was taken in Greenland (the land of the Big Ice) during the Ice Wisdom gathering of shamans and shamanic practitioners in 2009. Chapter 9 has more on the phenomenon and prophecy behind this gathering.

Shaman (pronounced *shah*-maan) is a word from the language of the Tungus people of Siberia and has been adopted widely by anthropologists to refer to persons in a great variety of non-Western cultures who were previously known by such terms as *witch, witch doctor, medicine man, sorcerer, wizard, magic man, magician,* and *seer.* A shaman is a man or woman who enters an altered state of consciousness—at will—to contact and utilize an ordinarily hidden reality in order to acquire knowledge and power, and to help other persons.[2] This name denotes shamans' ability to journey out of ordinary reality, space, and time, with discipline and purpose, into nonordinary reality, where they connect with energy and helping spirits to receive guidance, gain insight or power, or diagnose and treat illness. The term *seer* is often used to refer to shamans for the same reason. Through various methods of intention and trance, the shaman enters the nonordinary reality that exists just outside of our everyday perceptions. In part three, we'll look at nonordinary reality, the shamans' ability to journey there, and the intentions and trances they use to do so.

Shamanic seeing is different from ordinary seeing; it is a whole-body sensing and knowing that can, but does not always, include visual images. Shamans gather information and energy through what has been coined extrasensory perception (ESP). They receive visual images, feelings, insights, flashes, direct knowledge, telepathic messages, gut feelings, sensations, and direct experiences through all aspects and perception facilities of their mind, body, emotions, energy field, and soul.

Animism: the belief that all things are souls created from, filled with, and sustained by life-force energy

Shamans work diligently, on a daily basis, throughout their lives, to honor their spirit connections and to perfect their natural abilities to enter the nonordinary worlds of spirit for specific purposes, such as to gain insight, knowledge, or power; to obtain energy for healing, restoration, balance, or wholeness; or to find solutions to problems challenging their clients or the community. Nonshamans perceive that shamans enter into other dimensions of reality, time, and space. Therefore, shamans serve as intermediaries, messengers, and energy connections between the human world and the spirit worlds.

The Worlds According to Shamanism

We cannot separate the physical from the spiritual, the visible from the invisible. —Ted Andrews, *Animal Speak*

To the outsider or beginner, it may appear that shamans choose to live in two worlds at the same time. They consciously hold their awareness here in the ordinary, everyday world of physical matter as well as in the nonordinary world of spirit. The truth is, we all live in both worlds. Most of us are just not as aware of the other, less visible one as the shaman is. Seeing nonordinary reality is a natural ability available to all of us, but it's an ability that must be developed.

There is a common misunderstanding that the physical and spirit worlds are separate, when they are actually one and the same. What shamans call the spirit world does not exist in some other place, but is a part of our everyday reality, just outside of our usual perceptions.

Modern quantum physics has proven that there are, in fact, many worlds, dimensions, and realms that overlap and interact with one another. Much of the shaman's work is harnessing information and energies from these lesser-known worlds for practical use in our everyday world. Thus, shamans serve as bridges between the many other worlds.

The Great Web of Life: the vast web of energy connecting all things

For simplicity, I'll refer to two worlds: the everyday, ordinary, physical reality or world and the nonordinary reality or spirit world, with the understanding that the latter is actually a vast realm of infinite and indefinable energies and dimensions.

Animism and the Web of Life: Cornerstones of Shamanism

And I say the sacred hoop of my people was one of the many hoops that made one circle, wide as daylight and as starlight, and in the center grew one mighty flowering tree to shelter all the children of one mother and one father. —Black Elk, *Black Elk Speaks*

Shamans see the soul of the world in every rock, stream, bird, and cloud. This belief that all things are souls created from, filled with, and sustained by life-force energy is known as *animism*. It's the view that everything is alive and animated, even if it does not appear so. This book, the compost and plants in your garden, the trees, the mountains, the wind, the tarmac road, the rocks, the animals, the chair you are sitting in, you and me—all are animated souls.

In shaman traditions, we acknowledge that everything is living, filled with dynamic life-force energy, and connected to everything else by a web of energy called the Great Web of Life. This web itself is alive, spirited, animated, intelligent, accessible, mysterious, and divine. Some shamans see the web as a diffuse image of organized energy moving about like light smoke in the wind. Some shamans feel, sense, and experience the web as a force of energy.

Many shamans see and feel the Great Web of Life as a vast, infinite web or net of light-filled energy filaments connecting endless numbers of beings, who are also made of light and life-force energy.

The density, composition, and flow of life-force energy varies from being to being and filament to filament. We know that light is made up of a broad spectrum of frequencies, some of which we can see, some of which are invisible to us. The filaments of the web of life are similar to light in that some are very dense, having the appearance of a solid, physical form, while others are not and do not.

This life-force energy is a free-flowing, high-vibrational energy that shamans believe is the source—also referred to as *the Creator, Great Spirit,* or *God*—and is the foundation of everything. This energy is omnipresent and is the essence of all things, a subtle yet powerful undercurrent of all that is. Everything that exists is alive with life-force energy. This same life-force energy makes up the minute fibers of the web that links all things. The web of life radiates and pulses with this all-pervading energy.

In the ordinary world, manifestations of the web are visible as things such as beings, objects, and colors. Sounds, tastes, smells, and tingling sensations are also manifestations of the web, as are things considered to be extraordinary perceptions, like gut feelings, premonitions, intuition, and visions. Most people don't perceive the latter, the nonordinary-world manifestations of the web, with their five physical senses, since those manifestations are made of more subtle, less dense life-force energy. It is this less dense, subtle energy that shamans are trained to see, sense, feel, and experience through bare awareness, altered states of consciousness, and heightened sensory awareness. Bare awareness is the place within each person where the mind falls silent and inner knowing is all that exists.

> *Everything that exists is alive with life-force energy, a free-flowing, omnipresent, high-vibrational energy.*

In 1854, Chief Seattle, leader of the Suquamish and Duwamish tribes in what is now Washington State, very eloquently described the shamanic view of animism and the interconnectedness of the web of life:

> Every part of this soil is sacred in the estimation of my people. Every hillside, every valley, every plain and grove, has been hallowed by some sad or happy event in days long vanished. Even the rocks, which seem to be dumb and dead as they

swelter in the sun along the silent shore, thrill with memories of stirring events connected with the lives of my people, and the very dust upon which you now stand responds more lovingly to their footsteps than yours, because it is rich with the blood of our ancestors, and our bare feet are conscious of the sympathetic touch. Our departed braves, fond mothers, glad, happy hearted maidens, and even the little children who lived here and rejoiced here for a brief season, will love these somber solitudes and at eventide they greet shadowy returning spirits. And when the last Red Man shall have perished, and the memory of my tribe shall have become a myth among the White Men, these shores will swarm with the invisible dead of my tribe, and when your children's children think themselves alone in the field, the store, the shop, upon the highway, or in the silence of the pathless woods, they will not be alone. In all the earth there is no place dedicated to solitude. At night when the streets of your cities and villages are silent and you think them deserted, they will throng with the returning hosts that once filled them and still love this beautiful land. The White Man will never be alone.[3]

Bare awareness is the place within each person where the mind falls silent, and inner knowing is all that exists.

Let him be just and deal kindly with my people, for the dead are not powerless. Dead, did I say? There is no death, only a change of worlds. —Chief Seattle, 1854

Chapter 2

The Shaman's Companions: Helping Spirits

A shaman is never truly alone. Instead, there is an unwavering belief that loving companions are always traveling with us.

Evelyn C. Rysdyk,
teacher, healer, author

As we've already seen, shamans understand that everything that exists is made of and sustained by life-force energy and is interconnected by the energy of the Great Web of Life. This life-force energy is intelligent and omnipotent, formless and omnipresent. Ever since human beings became aware of the less-visible world around them, they have felt a need to identify this great force. Shamans, as well as yogis, esotericists, philosophers, spiritual authorities, and practitioners of all kinds, have referred to it by names that imply a vast and divine or spiritual power: Great Spirit, Great Mystery, Creator, Spirit, God, the Goddess, the Holy Spirit, Lord, Lady, Mother/Father God, Allah, prana, chi, ki, qi, Universal Power, the Higher Power, the Universal Source, the Light, the Source, the Divine, causal energy—the list goes on. For centuries, people have argued and fought over the names, but regardless of what it is called, this single life-force energy moves within every living thing. It is the spirit that moves in all things and imbues all things, whether those things are observably animate or inanimate, with the radiance of life. Many shamans refer to this energy as Great Spirit, so I will as well.

The all-pervading, divine life-force energy of Great Spirit has "assistant" energies, which are connected to it, each other, and everything that exists, including us, by the web of life. These assistant energies interact with us and act as bridges between us and the web and between us and the all-pervasive life force. These energies also take on particular energetic signatures and appearances that shamans can see, sense, feel, experience, and interact with in personal and tangible ways. Sometimes these energies manifest as personified images. These ambassadors of the web work with the shamans to bridge the worlds and to bring about harmony and balance within all of the worlds and their inhabitants. Shamans refer to these energies as helping spirits.

Shamans know that all worlds, ordinary and nonordinary, host an infinite number and variety of helping spirits. Shamans believe that everyone is born with at least one helping spirit that protects them and shares its power with them. Shamanic cultures also believe that a tribe, clan, or group has a spirit protector and ally, called a totem.

All worlds, ordinary and nonordinary, host an infinite number and variety of helping spirits.

Shamans affect healing and harmony in our ordinary world in order to ensure the survival and wellness of the people they serve: their clients, students, family, friends, community, and ultimately all of humanity, since all people on earth are connected by the web of life. They affect healing and harmony by collaborating with both their associates in the spirit world and their associates in the physical world, and by accessing the web of life for energy, healing, power, guidance, and wisdom. In fact, shamans believe they cannot do their sacred work without the direction, assistance, and cooperation of helping spirits. The painting *Fire Keepers,* shown in Figure 3, depicts the intimate connection that shamans experience with their helping spirits. It shows the shamans' sense that they and the spirits are one or are intertwined facets of one another.

Without helping spirits, a shaman would not be a shaman in the traditional sense. —Colleen Deatsman, *Seeing in the Dark*

Helping spirits are often invisible to the untrained person because they are composed of high-vibrating energy and are far less physically dense than we are. Because of esoteric study and quantum physics, we know the nature of their energy is subtle or etheric, and though their energetic vibrations are still much higher than our own, the energies of these helping spirits are more accessible than the highest-vibrating energies of all—those of Great Spirit.

The energy layers in which these helping spirits exist are called the subtle and causal levels of energy, though shamans often call them the spirit or etheric realms, or the nonordinary worlds of spirit. These nonordinary worlds and helping spirits actually aren't "out there"; they're right here, within

Figure 3

our physical, ordinary world. They're just vibrating at a higher frequency than most people perceive. Helping spirits are just the higher-vibrational, spiritual aspects of our everyday world, which means they are everywhere around us, all the time, just outside our ordinary, everyday, five-sense perception. They are of a lighter form of energy than people and physical objects are; to those who can perceive them, they glow with higher-vibrational energy. Shamans intentionally connect these higher-vibrating energies—these invisible aspects of our world—and the lower-vibrating, visible energies of our world.

Diverse Spirits, Diverse Names

These emissaries of the web of life are as diverse and unique as the rocks, flora, fauna, and humans we see and sense in our ordinary world. The term *helping spirit* encompasses many different forms and types of spirit energies. They can also be referred to as guardian spirits, spirit teachers, spirit healers, spirit allies, power animals, spirit guides, guardian angels, gods, goddesses, ascended masters, religious deities, ancestors, and deceased loved ones, depending upon the culture or religious orientation of the shaman perceiving them, the form the helping spirits exhibit, and their purpose. They may also be referred to by the names people use for certain energies, such as Christ consciousness, Goddess power, or nature guidance, or as archetypes with faces, bodies, shapes, forms, and names.

Helping spirits are higher-vibrational, spiritual aspects of our everydayworld, existing just outside our ordinary, five-sense perception.

Like the term *helping spirits*, most of these names are also broad titles used to identify a group of similar spirit energies. For example, the term *power animal* doesn't mean just helping spirits whose visual forms are four-legged, wild, furry land mammals, but also those who take the form of water mammals, domestic pets, birds, reptiles, amphibians, fish, and insects. The power shared by these beings is a spiritual power that has nothing to do with the size or strength of the being. In other words, a bear is no more or less powerful than a bee; their powers are simply different. All power animals are known to have powerful, helpful energies to offer the shaman.

The term *ascended masters* can include religious deities, but it also includes known and unknown masters of any discipline, such as artists, inventors, teachers, healers, saints, priests, priestesses, prophets, sages, yogis, gurus, hierophants, alchemists, or shamans who were once in human form on earth.

Nature is bursting with helpful energies and spirits. The terms *nature* and *elemental spirit* encompass faeries, elves, leprechauns, gnomes, the green man, and forest spirits, as well as the energies of air, fire, water, earth, and metal; rocks, stones, and crystals; trees and other plants; wind, clouds, and storms; the sun, moon, planets, and stars; and Mother Nature herself.

Mythical beings is a category of helping spirits that may appear as images such as unicorns, pegasuses, dragons, or griffins. Helping spirits that some shamans call angelic beings may appear as we would typically expect an angel to look, but they may also appear as energy beings without form, such as orbs of light or color, symbols, or geometric patterns. Nature spirits, such as faeries and gnomes, may also appear in these forms.

Helping spirits can also be called guardian spirits, spirit teachers, spirit healers, spirit allies, power animals, spirit guides, guardian angels, gods, goddesses, ascended masters, religious deities, ancestors, or deceased loved ones as well as Christ consciousness, Goddess power, or nature guidance.

As humans have explored consciousness, they have debated the nature of helping spirits. Traditional shamans view them as residents of our world accessible through nonordinary reality and entities who want to assist shamans with their work in this world. Some neo-shamans view helping spirits as facets of the shaman's soul or higher self. This view holds that shamans call upon the layers of their own soul, specifically those layers that resonate in the higher realms, then use these energies to draw power directly from the web to manifest change on this physical plane. The difference between these views is moot or a simple matter of semantics, because all shamans know there is no actual separation of beings or energies; we only think they are separate. To shamans, all helping spirits are parts of the oneness of all, just as the shaman is.

No matter what names or appearances helping spirits take, everyone can connect with them. Their "job" is to guide, protect, teach, and link us with the high vibration of the web of life, so we can glean energy, vitality, health, and wisdom. To connect with helping spirits, we must become aware of their presence, forge and honor relationships with them, and open ourselves to the high-powered energies. This is exactly what shamans do.

When shamans connect with their helping spirits, they tune in to and draw into themselves the high-vibrational energy of those spirits and the web. Shamans know that the more often they enter the nonordinary realities of higher-vibrational energies, the greater their capacity to operate at a higher-vibrational, or more spiritlike, level becomes. And increasing their capacity to work at this level, in turn, enables shamans to liberally travel the spirit worlds and garner more and more spiritual energy and power to utilize in service to the people.

When shamans connect with helping spirits, they tune in to and draw into themselves the high-vibrational energy of those spirits and the Great Web of Life.

Shamans also know that connecting with helping spirits and the web helps them remain energized and healthy. Renowned shamanism researcher, practitioner, and neo-shamanism pioneer Michael Harner has documented that connections to helping spirits increase one's physical energy to resist disease as well as mental alertness and self-confidence.[4]

In addition, spiritual energy is conscious and intelligent, and shamans can access it for guidance, wisdom, and knowledge; to elevate their own consciousness and that of others; to improve the quality of their lives and others' lives; and even to create miracles. This is not to say that spiritual energy is a panacea for life's struggles. Rather, it is a necessary and powerful tool for responding with strength, power, and direction to life's challenges.

Bonding with Spirits

To shamans, helping spirits are not only teachers and guides; they are allies, friends, soul-brothers, soul-sisters, soul-mates, and soul-family members. They are cherished companions. Often, shamans spend as much or more time with these partners as they do with their ordinary-world friends and families. More than a valued friendship, the connection with helping spirits is part and parcel of who the shaman is. Shamans feel responsible for nurturing, maintaining, and honoring these relationships.

Giving thanks to helping spirits is a very important part of shamans' life and practices. In so doing, they maintain harmony between themselves and their environment and the natural order. Many shamans use sacred tools and ceremonial offerings to express gratitude to the helping spirits. The puja dish, pictured in Figure 4, is an example of one such tool. Tibetan and Nepalese shamans use this ornate silver, turquoise, and wood cup to offer tea, milk, water, and grain to deities and spirits of the environment.

Figure 4

The Mutual Benefits of the Human-Spirit Relationship

Shamans understand that their special bond with helping spirits has mutual evolutionary and enlightenment benefits for both parties and both the ordinary and nonordinary worlds. The same energy that provides shamans with support, guidance, and power and preserves the well-being of the people also supports the helping spirits progress in their evolutionary process. Both humans and helping spirits are made from and made up of energy that is striving to become fully conscious itself. So in addition to working in harmony with humans out of compassion for the human experience, helping spirits work with humans to help people expand and raise their consciousness and energy vibrations. As people evolve, the helping spirits evolve, the web evolves, the whole world, the entirety of creation, evolves.

Helping spirits are always working with humans, even though humans may not always be aware of it.

Even the most minuscule shifts in consciousness register energetically, triggering advancement on all energetic levels.

Throughout history, helping spirits have worked with initiates—students, apprentices, and those engaged in shamanic self-study—even if the initiates are unaware and unenlightened. Helping spirits benefit as they assist initiates in becoming more aware and free of illusion. By sending initiates messages, which the initiates often view as coincidences, synchronicities, and omens, the spirits nudge and, when necessary, push initiates along their soul paths, rendering often unnoticed assistance and divine guidance.

When Spirits Speak

Shamans know that the helping spirits speak to them continually, not just when the shamans are within nonordinary reality, but also in everyday life. Spirits communicate in many different ways, so shamans pay attention, watching and listening for signs from animals and nature, as well as significant happenings in their day and interactions with others.

Helping spirits communicate in many different ways, so shamans watch and listen for signs from nature and within everyday life experiences.

For example, shamanic traditions teach that when an animal crosses your path, it would behoove you to study that animal. Within the animal's attributes, behaviors, colors, fundamental nature, and other characteristics are messages that guide shamans in their own situations or help in their work with the people. So shamans watch and study all of life's movements, paying close attention to things around them, such as animal behaviors, shifts in nature, changes in the weather, and the things people say. Paying close attention to all of life's movements can seem a bit overwhelming to the nonshaman to think about, and it may be difficult for shamans at first. But this skill soon becomes second nature to shamans.

Shamans believe that it is disrespectful and unfavorable to not pay attention to these messages. When people fail to acknowledge signs and omens or to take proper action in response to these signs, the messages will only get stronger, more noticeable, and more intense. They often start to take the form of challenging situations that make people feel increasingly uncomfortable until people to finally take notice and make appropriate changes. Things such as altercations in relationships, minor accidents, or illnesses are examples of these so-called cosmic two-by-fours. Shamans learn to pay attentions to subtle details, so they avoid the consequences of not noticing. They have learned that dealing with the effects of cosmic two-by-fours is a waste of precious energy when compared to the energy it takes to notice small, early signs and take action promptly.

By the very fact that we call upon God, the archangels, the invisible ones of Creation, they are there, and in our petition, they rush to us, that we might become aware of them. —Mark Stavish, *The Path of Alchemy*

Chapter 3

The Spirit of Nature and the Circle of Life

Forget not that the earth delights to feel your bare feet and the winds long to play with your hair.

Khalil Gibran, *The Prophet*

Nature

Shamans don't think about nature with an "us and them" mind-set. Shamans know that we, humans, are a part of nature, not exempt nor separate from the powers and effects of its forces.

In the history of humanity and shamanism, the challenges to survival were so difficult that most people were unable to perform any but the most essential life duties. Very few people had the time or penchant to ponder and explore the subtle balance of the spirits and energies of nature, and yet it was necessary that someone understand these forces to ensure survival. Therefore, these forces became the shaman's territory.

Early people depended on the shamans to understand and mediate the ever-present mysteries of nature. To these people, nature was often an adversary and destroyer, yet also a healer and sustainer of life. And nature was always family, for nature was home. Nature was, and is, omnipotent, and shamans then and now view it as a great force that demands to be addressed and honored.

To shamans, nature is an omnipotent force that demands to be addressed and honored.

Nature is the raw, untouched physical and energetic manifestation of the life-force energy and the web of life. Its two aspects, physical and energetic, swirl in tandem and overlap here in physical reality. To shamans, nature is alive, dynamic, and full of living beings—energies and forces that are visible and invisible, known and unknown. The visible and known aspects of nature and the web are the people, things, beings, and objects that most people see and sense as real and tangible. Even though these things appear to be, and are, physical, they are actually energy coalesced into a dense enough form that they have a sense of solidity. By honing their senses, shamans tune in to the invisible energies and forces—nature's subtler energy vibrations.

Honing the senses begins with the basic practice of awareness. You can practice awareness, too. For example, as you gaze at Figure 5, relax your mind, and simply notice what you sense and feel.

Every person can touch and witness the physical aspects of the web here, in this physical plane, by observing nature. Most people don't realize that when they observe the physical, they are often sensing the less obvious energetic aspects as well. The physical presence is what a thing

Figure 5

is. The energetic nature is what a thing *does.* Shamans are well aware of both the physical and energetic aspects of things and nature, and they know how to use both aspects to facilitate their work.

An example from plant spirit medicine teaches us that mullein is a tall, slender, attractive plant, with multitudes of tiny yellow blossoms, that grows wild in many parts of the world. Physically and energetically, mullein is a healer. Mullein is used to treat such physical issues as asthma, upper respiratory inflammation, constriction and cough, and diarrhea. The oil of mullein destroys disease-causing germs. It is widely used in teas and tinctures. Shamans may work with these physical aspects of mullein if they are spiritually guided to, but they may also enter into nonordinary reality to connect with the energy or spirit of the plant. If the spirit of the mullein is willing, it will share some of its energy and healing qualities with the shamans. The shamans gather this energy and direct it to the clients.

The shamans understand that this energy is a gift from the plant spirit, so they offer a gift of energy in return. Any spirit and nature energy the shamans accept and use must be balanced with energy given back. The ways shamans offer energy back to nature and spirit can be as grand as a special ceremony or as simple as a song of gratitude and reverence. Knowing that the balance must be maintained is vital to shamans' success.

Nature's Helping Spirits

Nature spirits are all of the energies and beings that live as the nonhuman inhabitants of the world, just outside of the ordinary perception of most people. Everything in nature is energy, and therefore, everything in nature is inspirited. Things such as rocks, trees, mountains, rivers, oceans, lakes, flora, fauna, wildlife, crystals, stars, planets, and the aurora borealis are all inspirited, so shamans view them as energies and beings, not just as things. Shamans refer to these energies and beings as nature spirits.

These nature spirits are pure sources of life-force energy that shamans can use to energize and revitalize an ailing client or community. Nature spirits are also teachers. They teach the shaman and the people about the impermanence of earthly life, the forces of creation and destruction, and

The physical presence is what a thing **is.**
The energetic nature is what a thing **does.**

the cycle of living, dying, and rebirth. These spirits communicate not only by speaking directly to the shaman, but also through actions. Every movement of the nature spirits is an expression of the character of this physical plane and of the universe, and as such, these movements are signs, omens, and portents containing potential knowledge for the shaman.

The energy found in nature is raw, primal power, and it exists and acts according to its fundamental makeup—not the prevailing social norms or attitudes. Its constant, unchanging nature allows it to be gathered and applied to any purpose.

Elemental Energies

The elements are perfect examples of nature spirits that can be potent shamanic allies, whose powers shamans can harness to foster harmony and balance, health and well-being, creation and destruction.

Shamans have long worked in concert with the elements: air, water, fire, and earth, and perhaps others such as metal, wood, and nature, depending upon the shaman's culture. All of nature comprises the subtle energies of the elements. Everything and every being, seen and unseen, known and unknown, is an element or, more accurately, a combination of elements in varying amalgamations.

> *Everything and every being, seen and unseen, known and unknown, is an element or combination of elements.*

For example, a thunderous ocean, a trickling waterfall, a babbling brook, and a placid lake are manifestations of the water element, whose energies shamans can tap and use. Figure 6, a photograph entitled *Spirit Speaks in Water Reflections* is an example of how one contemporary shaman is using water for healing. Photographer and shamanic practitioner Joy Markgraf shares, "After my awakening, the spirits taught me to look at reflections in water to create a beauty language that would speak to other people." By capturing the beauty of the water element on film, then sharing the images with others, Markgraf brings the energy of the water element to those people who need it.

A rumbling volcano, a bolt of lightning, the tepid summer sun, and a toasty campfire are expressions of the element of fire. A swirling tornado, a brisk breeze, and the soft voice of wind through the great oaks are some of the languages of the element of air. A rugged ice-capped mountain, luminous crystals, and warm, squishy clay are manifestations of the element of earth.

The energies of the elements express themselves in infinite ways and places, but to the shaman, these are not only individual expressions of energy, but also combinations of energies joining together in a dance of the balance and harmony of creation, destruction, and life. The water roll-

Figure 6

ing off the cliff (earth) mixes with air and sun (fire) to form a mist of rainbow prisms. The rugged, ice-capped mountain is a base of earth with fire at its core and frozen water at its peak, constantly being altered by internal shifts and high-altitude air currents. Each combination of elements forms a unique energy and set of circumstances. Ask anyone who has stood under a waterfall rainbow or attempted to climb a mountain 12,000 feet or higher. Shamans can tap in to these confluences of elemental nature energies and use the elements' combined power to help shift stagnant energies in a client or a village.

Shamans can harness and use the powers of individual elements or of combinations of elements.

The Energies of Directions and Places

Like the elements, the directions are composed of infinite and varied energies and spirits that assist shamans in their work of service. The number of directions acknowledged and the powers associated with each direction vary widely across traditions and cultures. Some honor and address the four cardinal directions of east, south, west, and north. Most also honor and address the directions of above and below. In addition to these six directions, many shamans acknowledge the directions of center, circle, and within. Shamanic traditions worldwide believe that center is a direction of power because people are the center of their own lives and are a part of nature; thus, by acknowledging the power of the direction of center, people honor and acknowledge themselves as a part of the circle of power.

Just as shamans call upon the spirits of specific animals, rocks, trees and plants, and stars for knowledge and assistance, so do they call upon the spirits of specific locations—power places or energy vortexes. Traditional shamanic stories teach that spirits live in or near sacred trees, mountains, springs,

> *Just as shamans call upon the spirits of specific animals, rocks, trees and plants, and stars for knowledge and assistance, so do they call upon the spirits of power places and energy vortexes.*

valleys, hills, oceans, streams, lakes, and forests. These sacred places are home to all manner of spirits and may host multiple entities from different times and with varying characteristics. Mount Shasta, Machu Picchu, the Ganges River, the Grand Canyon, and Sedona, Arizona's Airport Mesa and Bell Rock vortexes are examples of places where specific energies and spirits are known to reside. Shamans know that the spirits of places like these are so powerful that they change the vibrations of the energy fields of all who enter their sphere of influence. These spirits communicate with shamans not only with words but also with actions and movements that promptly create energetic and physical shifts. It may be that these power places are sites where the grid lines—channels of energy that circle the globe, often called ley and dod lines—intersect or converge. Regardless of what gives the energies of these places their strength, shamans know, feel, and sense these powerful energies and use them in their work.

Every culture includes stories of shamans undertaking lengthy, hazardous treks to revered power places in order to make gestures of honor to the resident spirits and to request wisdom, healing, insight, power, and transformation from them. Often, shamans must demonstrate great presence of mind and focused devotion to their purpose in order to survive the interaction. The power of these spirits of place is thought to be daunting, and the scope of their knowledge so vast and beyond that of their supplicant, that without a singular purity of purpose, the shaman would succumb to the rigors of the journey or the interaction with the entity.

These journeys and interactions with the spirits of place are often used to test neophyte shamans. Making such a journey and encountering these spirits are only two of possibly several challenges these seekers of wisdom and energy must surpass if they are to serve their people with impeccability. Clarity of mind, focused intention, awareness of detail, and accurate choices often mean the difference between each shaman's life or death in these stories. If the shamans succeed in making the journey, encountering the spirits and facing the challenges presented, the resident spirits bestow on them power and knowledge, which the shamans can use for themselves and their people. Shamans always accept these gifts with a humble heart and deep gratitude.

> *If the sight of the blue sky fills you with joy, if a blade of grass springing up in the fields has power to move you, if the simple things in nature have a message you understand, rejoice, for your soul is alive.* —Eleanora Duse

The Circle of Life

> *You have noticed that everything an Indian does is in a circle, and that is because the Power of the World always works in circles, and everything tries to be round.* —Black Elk, *Black Elk Speaks*

Shamans know that life—all of life: nature, humans as components of nature, helping spirits, energy, ordinary and nonordinary reality—moves in circles, spirals, and cycles. Within life, there are infinite circles, and circles within circles, since energy is neither created nor destroyed, but simply recycled.

The very underpinning of life is a conglomeration of natural energies and worlds that operates in infinite seen and unseen, known and unknown circles. The building block of life, unseen until the advent of modern science, is the spherical atom, made up of even smaller circles: protons, electrons, neutrons. Atoms combine to form round molecules, which coalesce to form circular cells. The intelligence of our cells, our DNA, is a circular spiral. Our entire body is an infinite conglomeration of circles.

Circles are evident everywhere in nature. The earth is a sphere that encircles the globular sun in an orbit that generates sunrise and sunset rotations and seasonal cycles. Coyotes dig circular dens to give birth to pups formed by the union of circular cells. Flowers bloom in a circular display of petals that sprout from a round center. Birds build circular nests and lay rounded eggs.

Life is a cyclical journey, not a linear one—an ongoing, dynamic circle of birth, growth, death, and rebirth on every level: spiritual, energetic, emotional, mental, and physical.

Life is a cyclical journey, not a linear one—an ongoing, dynamic circle of birth, growth, death, and rebirth on every level: spiritual, energetic, emotional, mental, and physical. Challenges arise and are addressed or not. Spiritual lessons arrive and are learned or not. Energies are garnered, utilized, and released. Emotions rise and fall; thoughts form, grow, and dissipate. Cells generate, function, and terminate. Life is born into the ordinary world, and at some point, the body dies, and the soul energy reenters the nonordinary worlds. This is the circle of life according to the shaman. All things are living beings that have circular life cycles.

Shamans perceive the web of life as an enormous circle comprising infinite interconnected circles of constantly cycling and recycling energies. Circles can be ambiguous since they have no beginning, no middle, and no end. Circles are energy in motion, a constant flow of life-force energy. To the shaman, this flow is power and, therefore, worth paying close attention to.

The medicine wheel, used in many shamanic cultures throughout the world, is both a representation of and a sacred tool for accessing the power of the cyclical, interconnected nature of all things. Every living being has a personal medicine wheel

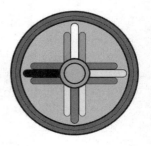

Figure 7

within and around it, generally just outside of ordinary awareness, that the shaman can tap in to for assistance when needed. A personal medicine wheel is a circle of power that connects each being to all other circles, and circles within circles, of the web. It is a tangible microcosm of the universe that the trained shaman can see, feel, sense, experience, and use through awareness, focus, and intent.

Physical representations of medicine wheels exist in many cultures in multitudes of forms, such as the ancient stone formation and artwork shown in Figures 7 and 8. Figure 7 is an artistic representation of the medicine wheel with four sacred colors, representing certain properties, attributes, characteristics, powers, medicines, energies, directions, seasons, and life cycles, that change around the wheel. Color configurations can vary based on the culture and tradition.

Figure 8 is a picture of the Big Horn Medicine Wheel located in the Big Horn Mountains outside of Lovell, Wyoming. This wheel is believed to be eight hundred years old and to have been used by several different indigenous peoples over the years.

Most physical medicine wheels have a basic pattern that begins with the center stone, or cairn, from which spokes of stone radiate to an outer ring of stones. Larger stones or cairns are typically placed at

Figure 8

the four cardinal directions. Stone medicine wheels are sacred gathering places that shamans utilize for ceremony, prayer, meditation, teaching, and healing. Humans are spirits, divine energy in human form, connected to all other energies. The circular medicine wheel signifies this connection, and it functions as a vortex or sphere of power, which shamans use as a contact point from which to bridge this world and all other worlds, ordinary and nonordinary. By honoring the medicine wheel and the circles of life, shamans honor their relationships with helping spirits and the Great Spirit within themselves. Shamans know that nothing is separate, that everything is one, so when they honor the Great Spirit within themselves, they are honoring the Great Spirit in all, the holistic nature of all that is.

When we die, our bodies become the grass, and the antelope eat the grass. And so we are all connected in the great Circle of Life.
—Mufasa, *The Lion King*

The Hollow Bone

Part Two

Who
Are
Shamans?

Chapter 4

The Many Faces of Shamanism

My father died about twenty years ago. Nearly fifteen years later, when I was about fifty, my father began to come to me in dreams. He brought his power to me. He told me to doctor. I dreamed about him three or four times before I believed that I would doctor. After awhile, the power started to come to me when I dreamed. Then I stopped dreaming about my father. The rattlesnake told me what to do. The snake helps me doctor now. It comes to me when I dream.

Rosie Plummer, quoted in *Shamanic Voices* by Joan Halifax

As stated in chapter 1, the term *shaman* is a borrowed term originating in Siberia and denoting a person's ability to perform certain actions, such as journeying into nonordinary reality, communing with spirits, and understanding and harnessing the energies of nature. In *Awakening to the Spirit World,* Sandra Ingerman and Hank Wesselman tell us, "The truth is that humans everywhere share basic traits, abilities, and skills with shamans—visionaries who simply develop these skills to a masterful degree through their initiations and subsequent training. Although shamanic abilities usually remain latent in many people, everyone can make use of the shamanic approach to

41

life because it is natural and basic to all humans everywhere on the planet. All humans have intuitive abilities at some level."[5]

Shamans' actions and thoughts are what makes them shamans. In traditional shamanic cultures, shamans do not call themselves shamans (or any related term); the community calls them shamans, if and when they regularly and accurately perform the duties their community requires of a shaman and performs them to the community's standards. Shamans, both traditional and neo-shamans, are known in their communities, and it is the community that ultimately decides if shamans are being effective in their work. A shaman who produces consistent, effective results that help people and the community is a busy shaman.

Shamans in the twenty-first century basically fit into one of the four following groups, which share some similar beliefs and practices, but in other ways are very different from each other:

- Traditional indigenous shamans (and their indigenous apprentices)

- Nonindigenous people trained in traditional shamanism by traditional indigenous shamans

- Core-shamanism practitioners

- Indigenous and nonindigenous people trained in both traditional shamanism (by traditional indigenous shamans) and core-shamanism

Traditional Indigenous Shamans

The God Saub spoke from the sky
He threw down the sacred bamboo wood
We call that "bamboo shaman"
Whoever lifts it up
Will lead the life of the shaman
And will have power to heal . . .
Sometimes an old man gets weaker and weaker and dies
His soul climbs the steps to the sky
You must follow the soul to the sky when you shake
You follow the path to the sick one
If the weak soul goes to the sky
Maybe it just wants to die

It goes to the ancestral family in the sky
The soul goes to the place where it can get release
And power to be born again
And passage to another life . . .
Saub gives you power to help the soul
To catch and protect the soul
If you follow this way
Truly you can catch the soul
And the sick one will feel better
You go to catch the soul with your two hands
And with your heart
And you grip the soul
After that, the sick one feels better too . . .

—Paja Thao, "The Shaman,"
from *I Am a Shaman*

Traditional shamans in most parts of the world, throughout history, have been misunderstood, misinterpreted, ridiculed, disenfranchised, removed from the people, and exterminated. In his *Pocket Guide to Shamanism*, teacher and author Tom Cowan tells us,

"When Western travelers and explorers first encountered shamans in tribal cultures, they did not know what to make of them. . . . Usually the shaman's helping spirits were misinterpreted by Christian observers as 'evil spirits' or 'demons.' When viewed in modern mental-health terms, shamans seemed sick, delusional, or outright crazy. A shaman talks to trees, rocks, and other supposedly 'nonintelligent' entities and claims to have magical powers to shapeshift into other forms, to visit invisible realms, and to consort with the dead."[6]

Traditional shamans are men and women of indigenous heritage who have answered the calling from spirit to become a shaman, have satisfactorily completed the training requirements determined by their culture, and are practicing their shamanic work with consistent results. In 1944, anthropologist Alfred Métraux defined shamans as "any individual who maintains by profession and in the interest of the community an intermittent commerce with spirits, or who is possessed by them."[7]

Beliefs about shamans and their abilities are diverse and vary from culture to culture. Many cultures believe their shamans have supernatural powers that can heal or harm, as well as extraordinary abilities and individualized knowledge. Shamans are often considered to be spiritual leaders or priests or priestesses. They can enter into a trance state at will, allowing their souls to leave their body and enter the invisible worlds. Shamans view animal images as power animals, spirit protectors, guides, and message-bearers.

The role of shaman can also encompass a wide range of services and duties, which, like beliefs about shamans, vary from shaman to shaman and culture to culture. Roles and functions the traditional shaman may assume include:

- Divining information, wisdom, and knowledge from the ordinary and nonordinary worlds

- Leading ceremonies

- Acting as an intermediary between the invisible spirit world and the people in order to restore health, drive out unhelpful evil spirits, and ensure success in hunting, gathering, and agricultural endeavors

- Preparing the people for hunting, gathering, and agricultural efforts

- Communicating with the spirits and divining guidance about hunting, gathering, and agricultural matters

- Seeing the future

- Recognizing and reading signs and omens

- Officiating rites of passage, training, and ceremonies

- Locating and bringing back wandering souls

- Retrieving lost power and soul parts

- Communicating with the dead

- Influencing the weather

- Removing possessing spirits, evil spirits, and souls who have not crossed over from a person, family, group of people, or place

- Performing sacrifices to appease the spirits and the gods,
- Using plants, plant energies, and plant spirits for healing purposes
- Talking to nature spirits, such as the helping spirits of plants, animals, rocks, water, and weather elements
- Singing songs to invoke, connect with, and honor helping spirits
- Singing healing songs
- Diagnosing illnesses
- Learning and exploring universal laws and the ways of energy and power
- Teaching apprentices and the people certain spiritual ways
- Setting bones, pulling teeth, treating wounds
- Adjusting the physical body using techniques such as massage and manipulation (similar to adjustments done by an osteopath or chiropractor)
- Channeling life-force, spiritual, elemental, and personal energy through hands-on healing
- Interpreting dreams
- Delivering babies
- Performing energy work
- Conducting soul-crossings to the spirit world (psychopomp)
- Counseling, advising, and mediating for individuals, couples, families, and groups when guidance or conflict resolution is needed
- Invoking helping spirits to protect them from the rigors of their craft and the risks taken during arduous training and when working with clients or the community, enemy shamans or sorcerers, the spirit world, transient energies, and toxins from entheogens (psychoactive substances)

Parts three and four describe many of these activities in more detail.

The people of traditional shamanic cultures look to their shamans to help them navigate the omnipresent challenges and ambiguities of nature, life, and relationships by communicating with the spirits of the ordinary and nonordinary realities. Because of the shamans' much valued and unique role in the community, and because of the power shamans hold, people often fear, honor, and protect them.

While the shaman plays an essential role in the life of the people, shamans in traditional shamanic cultures may live separately from the people, such as in a nearby forest or at the far edge of the village, but shamans may also live among the people, within villages, towns, and cities. As in all things shamanic, where a shaman chooses to live depends on the individual shaman and the needs of the people.

Traditional shamans are men and women of indigenous heritage who have answered the calling from spirit, have satisfactorily completed the training requirements determined by their culture, and are practicing their shamanic work with consistent results.

In many cultures, shamans may absent themselves from the people for periods of time. The shamans' need to maintain high levels of connection with spirit and openness to the forces of nature and the universe may pull them into seclusion or solitude from time to time. Shamans are specialists at walking between the ordinary and nonordinary worlds and, in most cases, can just as easily walk between the worlds of solitude and human busyness. In some instances, though, their need for solitude makes it difficult for shamans to live among the people, which is why shamans may live near, but not among, communities and come and go as guided by spirit and needed by the people.

In some traditional shamanic cultures, one or several primary shamans do all of the different kinds of shamanic work the people need, including healing, ceremonies, counseling, death rites, and escorting souls to the spirit realms. In other cultures, specific types of shamans fulfill specific roles and perform specialized functions. For example, among the Nanai people of Siberia, a distinct kind of shaman acts as a psychopomp, or person who guides souls to the afterlife.[8] Other shamans may be distinguished by the type of spirits or realms of the spirit world with which they most commonly interact.

In traditional shamanism, it is believed that different types of shamans view the world in very different ways, and those views determine their roles in society. José Stevens tells us in *Awakening to the Spirit World*, "[A]ll of these societies have five distinct classes of shamans . . ."[9] He explains that the first class is the shamans who practice the dark arts and harmful acts, such as sending intrusions and curses, causing illnesses, and invoking spirit to bring injury or bad luck to others.

Beliefs in witchcraft and sorcery also thrive in many traditional shamanic cultures. Some cultures differentiate shamans that heal and serve the good of the people from sorcerers who harm or serve only themselves, while others claim that all shamans have the power to both cure and kill. Often there is some debate about whether someone is a shaman or a type of sorcerer.

A good example of this debate is Carlos Castaneda. Though his books appear in the genre of shamanism and many cultures would call Castaneda a shaman, many others would not consider him a shaman because he trained with a man of knowledge to be a man of knowledge, instead of becoming a healer or helper to the people. A man of knowledge seeks wisdom and understanding of the spirit realms and

In some cultures, one or several primary shamans do all the different kinds of shamanic work the people need. In other cultures, specific types of shamans fulfill specific roles and perform specialized functions.

mysteries of life so that he can ultimately transcend the cycle of living, dying, and rebirth, rather than using this knowledge for healing and being of service to others. Some would say he was a sorcerer, not in a black-magic way (unless others were hurt) but in the sense that he "sourced" the spirit world for knowledge to help him with his own self-fulfilling or selfish purpose. Others would say, yes, Castaneda practiced shamanism.

The second class of shamans, says Stevens, are those who never innovate because they believe they must do everything in strict accordance with their training. The third class comprises the shamans who demand to be all powerful; these shamans can be more innovative, but only if innovation boosts their reputation and rewards. In the fourth class are the shamans dedicated to the service of others. Their ability to help and connect with others is of utmost importance to them. The fifth class consists of the shamans dedicated to their relationships with helping spirits and to being of assistance to others, but who are also innovative, individualized, exploration minded, and able to wield great powers.

Additionally, traditional shamans experience different callings, which determine the services they perform and roles they fulfill. Their purpose and their services may shift over their lifetime. Some shamans are called to work with all issues and concerns—individual, community, and global—that face their people. Some shamans may be called to focus on helping individual people with emotional discord, unhealthy patterns and imprints, energy imbalances and intrusions, or soul and power loss. Other shamans may be called to doctor people with physical health issues, illness, injury, and disease. Some shamans are called to focus on the community, tribe, clan, family, neighborhood, or friends; the work of these shamans might be more counseling and mediation oriented, or they may attend to the rites of passage and ceremonial needs of the community.

The community-focused shaman may use "seeing" and divination to ensure safe and successful journeys and hunts or to garner protection for the community at specific times, such as when it's facing hostilities or moving to a different location. The community-focused shaman may use dreaming to gain guidance and insight about what innovations the community can implement to ensure harmony and balance within the community, between it and other communities, and between the people and nature.

For many shamans, especially in modern times, their community has become the world.

For many shamans, especially in modern times, their community has become the world. Shamans have always regarded the world as part of the community they serve, but modern shamans' connection to the greater world is much more obvious. And it's easier for shamans to come together now, due to technology. As global communication becomes increasingly easy, traditional shamans around the world can work together to address healing, com-

Figure 9

munity, and world issues. Internet groups and forums have become places where shamans and shamanic practitioners around the globe can share healing techniques, insights, stories, prayer, and solutions to global and community issues.

One example of traditional shamans gathering for a common purpose is the International Council of Thirteen Indigenous Grandmothers, pictured in Figure 9. Formed in 2004, this group of shamanic elders from all over the world comes together in various locations to teach peace, compassion, and love. The council's intention is to combine prayer, education, and healing to help address the growing concerns of earth and its people during this time of great change.

Nonindigenous People Trained by Traditional Indigenous Shamans

In Lakota we don't have words like ownership or soul. When I sit here, I see another world than you do—a world of relationship. To me, all objects are active. For example, we don't say chair or table. Our equivalent is "chairing" and "tabling." They are alive—and doing what they are supposed to do. We don't own. How can you own earth? We have a responsibility to take care of mother earth, to live "with" it, not "on" it. I held on to my own identity by metaphorical thinking. I beheld my dreams, my visions, and intuition, as opposed to a system based rationally on shame, guilt, sin, hope, and illusions like money. I can't let go of the ancient ways. —Tiokasin Ghosthorse, host and producer of First Voices Indigenous Radio

Today, many nonindigenous and indigenous people are connecting with shamanic teachers of different cultures. Innovations in the technology of travel over the past fifty years or so have made it possible for apprentices and students to travel worldwide to learn from traditional indigenous shamans, and for traditional indigenous shamans to travel to teach students and apprentices far from their homelands. In addition, the Internet has made it possible for apprentices and students to communicate online with traditional indigenous shamans.

Neo-shamanism *is the term for a new type of revitalized shamanism based on the common values, philosophies, and practices of shamanism traditions around the world.*

These new ways of connecting allow students to learn shamanic ways of living, thinking, being, and healing from teachers and cultures they would have never been able to connect with in the past (at least not in the physical, ordinary reality). This revolution has facilitated increased interest in and growth of shamanism around the globe.

One example of these modern cross-cultural connections is shaman and teacher Marco Nuñez Zamolloa, who brought the wisdom teachings and medicine ways of his home, the Peruvian Andes, to the Condor Meets the Eagle conference in Canada in September 2010. There he met with teacher and shamanic practitioner Martha Lucier of Shamanism Canada, a welcoming sanctuary for shamanism students and teachers who wish to enhance their shamanism practice by learning, sharing, and practicing with others. (Shamanism Canada is an off-shoot of Northern Edge Algonquin, a training and retreat facility near Algonquin Provincial Park, Ontario, Canada.) Zamolloa and Lucier are pictured in Figure 10.

The roles and functions of these new shamans and practitioners trained by traditional indigenous are as varied as those of their traditional shamanic teachers. What responsibilities these new shamans and practitioners take on depends on the individual practitioner; his or her culture, community, and clients; and the teacher(s) he or she trained with.

Core-Shamanism Practitioners: Western Neo-Shamanism

Neo-shamanism is a term for a new type of revitalized shamanism that is based on the common values, philosophies, and practices found at the core of all traditional shamanism around the world. Practitioners of neo-shamanism are both indigenous and nonindigenous people, working to bring the core elements of shamanism into practice in all cultures in the twenty-first century. Due to significant cultural changes brought on by such phenomena as genocide, colonization, and globalization, many traditional shamans have been killed, scattered, and forced to severely limit their shamanic activities or to practice them secretly. These radical changes resulted in a relatively sudden loss of shamanic knowledge and practice.

Figure 10

One of the goals of the neo-shamanism movement is to support the return of shamanism to traditional communities and countries where it has been lost or fragmented. Additionally, neo-shamans practice shamanic techniques and live the philosophies of shamanism no matter where they live.

The call to be a shaman, a shamanic practitioner, or a neo-shaman hasn't changed in thousands of years. When we are called, we are called. Whether or not we answer that call is up to us.

Like many, I was called as a child. For as long as I can remember, I have experienced unexplainable healing abilities, sensitivities, visions, dreams, intuition, and extrasensory perceptions. But I did not grow up in a shamanic culture; I grew up in a rural, mostly Caucasian, middle-class, conservative, Republican, Christian world. Though I was deeply loved, I felt a loss that had no cultural reference. I didn't understand the feelings, sensations, experiences, and dreams I had, and there was no one I could ask for help. I didn't think my parents would understand what I was experiencing (though now I know better), and the clergy in my world, with one exception very early on, were unreachable. Nature was our family connection and my sacred teacher, so I took my questions to her, sitting quietly, waiting, and absorbing.

The roles and functions of both traditional shamans and neo-shamans vary widely, depending on the individual practitioner and his or her culture, community, clients, and teachers.

Years later, my life was going fine, or so I thought, until, as I shared in the introduction, the onset of an illness that the medical community didn't understand or have the ability to treat. My desire to fight and beat that illness ignited my inner warrior and spurred me to learn of a new way of life, which changed everything for me. That new way of life was living shamanically. Training in core-shamanism brought me guidance as well as an understanding of the philosophy and techniques of living shamanically.

Like the roles and functions of traditional shamans, those of these shamanic practitioners vary widely depending on the individual practitioner and on his or her culture, community, clients, and teachers.

Underneath the cultural flavors unique to each traditional shamanic community are common practices, knowledge, and beliefs that are of value in any culture. Like traditional shamans, neo-shamans believe in animism, the web of life, and they work with energies, helping spirits, and the nonordinary-reality spirit worlds, which they enter by shifting into an altered state of consciousness called trance. Repetitive drumming, shaking a rattle, intoning sounds or vowels, singing, chanting, dancing, or ingesting entheogens help shamans enter that trance state.

There are mixed thoughts about neo-shamanism, especially within traditional shamanic cultures. Some traditional shamans are wary of neo-shamanism, feeling that their healing and spiritual ways are being imitated or appropriated by people who do not have the cultural understanding or appropriate depth and types of training to practice shamanism. Whether or not modern shamanic practitioners receive enough hands-on guidance and supervision from their teachers is also a question. Additionally, some people are concerned about neo-shamanic practitioners offering fraudulent services and ceremonies or practicing shamanism with malicious intentions.

On the other hand, many people, including many from traditional shamanic cultures, support neo-shamanism. They see the connection between all peoples, and they herald cultures coming together for the benefit of all people and the world. They see the pain and suffering of the human experience and believe that more shamanism will help, not hinder, efforts to address them. Many prophecies, such as the Prophecy of the Meeting of the Eagle and the Condor, shared by many cultures around the world; the Seventh Fire Prophecy of the Anishinaabe people; and the Hopi Prophecy, as well as predictions about 2012 from the Mayans, Nostradamus, and many practitioners of Western mysticism traditions, speak of a union of people on earth and the shifting of the spiritual vibrations toward a vibration of oneness.

Underlying the cultural flavors unique to each traditional shamanic community are common practices, knowledge, and beliefs that are of value in any culture.

Indigenous and Nonindigenous People Trained in Both Traditional Shamanism and Core-Shamanism

In modern times, there has been a revival of shamanism, as people of all genders, cultures, creeds, and ethnic backgrounds around the world awaken, receive the calling from spirit and their soul, or crave meaning, healing, soulfulness, spirit connection, nature, and direct guidance. From this resurgence several new groups of shamans have sprung. These nontraditional shamans are commonly called shamanic practitioners and may be trained in various ways, by various teachers. They practice what is called combination shamanism—a combination of core-shamanism and indigenous shamanic techniques.

A large number of people are now being trained in traditional shamanism by traditional indigenous shamans and in core-shamanism through many available programs, workshops, and apprenticeships.

Again, the roles and functions of these shamanic practitioners are as varied as those of the traditional shaman and depend on the individual practitioner; his or her culture, community, and clients; and the teachers he or she trained with. Each student of shamanism is unique. Students have widely varied purposes, functions, beliefs, and spirit-guided requirements for the training they receive. Some find one teacher of a particular culture or with a certain way of working, and they feel deeply satisfied working with this one teacher. Others are drawn to seek out a variety of teachers to learn many techniques, cultural understandings, and applications of shamanism. Some work with indigenous teachers and are then drawn to augment their training with core-shamanism, while others may begin with core-shamanism and augment their learning by studying or apprenticing with indigenous teachers. In some cases, shamanic students find that fully immersing themselves in a shamanic culture outside of their own helps them to accept and use their shamanic gifts and teachings.

One such example comes from my colleague Shilo Satran, who has trained with several different shamanic teachers, first through the Foundation for Shamanic Studies in the United States and then later with a Sangoma Shaman in Swaziland, Africa.

"For me, the training in core-shamanism was like going to college and taking classes towards a degree," Satran says. "My time in Africa with P. H. Mtshali (a Zulu Sangoma) was like getting your first job after you've graduated: you've seen the material before, but college doesn't really train you for the job; it just proves you're teachable."

She continues:

I found myself in Africa, and from the moment I agreed to go, it was clear that the spirits were in charge. So many obstacles came up that were then easily cleared after I did a ceremony. Being on the homestead was like nothing I had ever experienced before. There was no running water. I slept in a sleeping bag in a cement floor. The nearest store was over an hour away. To eat chicken meant picking a live bird out of a cage from a vendor, taking it home, killing it, plucking it, eviscerating it, and finally cooking it. My life was flipped upside down and turned inside out. Relationship with my ancestor spirits really was the only priority.

My time in Africa has definitely changed my life. I have a deep relationship with the spirits and my ancestors that I work to develop and deepen on a daily basis. I understand, at a very fundamental level, that shamanism is about relationship: relationship with myself, relationship with my family, relationship with all living beings, and relationship with the natural world as well as relationship with the spirit world and my ancestors. And in order to manifest a healing or a dream, I have to be in right relationship with all of them. Right relationship comes from focus, intent, and a daily spiritual practice. Since my time in Africa, shamanism really has become a way of being. I'm connected more to my higher self and my ancestors, living to manifest what is in my highest good as well as that of all my relations and Mother Earth.[10]

What Do Shamans Look Like?

Often, people think about Native Americans as we were envisioned at the turn of the century. If we're not walking around in buckskin and fringe, mimicking the stereotype in dress and art form, we're not seen as real. Native Americans are here, and we are contemporary people, yet we are very much informed and connected to our history. —Charlene Teters, artist, activist, and lecturer

For many people, the term *shaman* conjures old-movie images of Indians, or they think of an old indigenous man shaking a rattle over an ailing client, a medicine woman tending to a new birth, or a young male apprentice with wild eyes dancing around the fire while dressed in ceremonial regalia of leather and feathers, brightly colored woven fabric, or animal

continued on the next page

furs. These images may or may not be accurate. Throughout history and now today, a shaman's appearance and dress depends on the individual shaman, his or her spirit guidance, and the cultural customs and expectations of the people the shaman serves. Shamans generally wear the dress of their culture or clothing expected of their role.

Figure 11

For example, Figure 11 shows the late Thomas Banyacya Sr., a contemporary Hopi elder, messenger, and teacher of peace. Banyacya is wearing the common attire of Hopi men. The dress is functional and practical while having a dressed-up appearance. Hopi men wear 100 percent cotton clothing that is handwoven and detailed with colors, patterns, and designs, and jewelry traditional to the Hopi culture. The turquoise and shells used to make this necklace were obtained from various tribes through trading, and the Hopi consider the silver necktie to be "cowboy redneck" attire. (Banyacya's son explained, "Some white people like to dress up like the Indians; some Indians like to dress up like the cowboys.") It is hot in the desert, so the red scarf acts as a sweatband to keep sweat and hair away from the face.

The rattle Banyacya holds is made of gourd, an important component of tools in Hopi life. In addition to rattles, gourds are used for many things, including scoops, spoons, and water vessels. The gourd rattle is important in Hopi tradition and ceremony. It is used to alert the people or spirits in the otherworlds that something is about to happen. This particular rattle is a male rattle, bearing an abstract drawing symbolizing a male person. The four bent lines connected at the center rotate to the left and symbolize the rotation of everything in the universe. This symbol is encircled by what looks like a ring of fire, representing the sun's rays. The rattle itself is an image or representation of light.

Figure 12

In Figure 12, a Urarina shaman, of the indigenous people of the Peruvian Amazon Basin, is wearing the common clothing of his culture, along with specific accoutrements—a necklace, body adornments, and a colorful woven, feathered headdress—that signify he is a shaman.

In most shamanic cultures and practices, dress is important to both the shaman and the people. A shaman's dress indicates his or her position and responsibilities within the community, and it is an honor to wear the attire signifying the position of a shaman. More important, at least to shamans, is that their dress honors and represents Spirit manifested in the physical. By wearing specific Spirit-guided colors, objects, or fabrics, shamans open the connection to nonordinary, spirit worlds and establish a channel for energy exchange.

Figure 13 shows the late Pau Karma Wang Chuk, a Tibetan shaman of Nepal, in full shamanic ceremonial dress, playing the big *nga chen* (also known as the lama drum). The headdress wings are like the rainbow on which

Figure 13

the ascetic saint Milarepa ascended to the top of Mt. Kai-lash. In this picture, Wang Chuk was a very old man, but he was only a teenager when he was initiated as a shaman in Tibet. In the 1950s, the Chinese invaded Tibet, and Wang Chuk fled to Nepal, along with many other Tibetans.

No matter the source of the training, be it traditional, modern, in dreams, or through experiences, the outcome is the same: the shaman dies to their old ways of thinking and acting and lives in ecstatic connection with Spirit and the web of life. It can be said that nothing changes, yet everything changes because the shaman's perspective on life and what is real is dramatically shifted through their trainings, initiations, and work in service of others. It is precisely this phenomenon of shamanic death and rebirth that makes a shaman a hollow bone, and thus markedly different from their neighbors and community.

The Hollow Bone

Chapter 5

Answering the Call: Becoming a Shaman

Inside each and every one of us is our one, true authentic swing. Something we was born with. Something that's ours and ours alone. Something that can't be learned. Something that's got to be remembered.

Bagger Vance, *The Legend of Bagger Vance*

Studying shamanism, learning shamanic techniques, and engaging in shamanic training, activities, and ceremonies does not make one a shaman. Becoming a shaman requires a deep, undeniable spirit calling (external or internal); intense self-exploration; numerous, arduous initiations; and a lifetime dedication to studying, training, apprenticing, experiencing, healing, and practicing. It is no easy undertaking and one that few ever consider.

"Shamanism, becoming a shaman and living as a shaman is a difficult and demanding life path that many indigenous people shy away from because of the formidable requirements. . . ." Tom Pinkson, shaman and transpersonal psychologist, writes on his website.

"Shamanism is not about fun and glamour. Unskillful and uneducated acts can cause harm, or even be life-threatening, to the shamanic practitioner as well as others. Shamanism deals with power, and power can move in many different ways, like electricity. It is important to move slowly with respect, humility, and care when practicing shamanism."[11]

The Calling

> *I became a shaman not cause it was my will*
> *But because it was the will of my shaman spirits*
> *The shaman spirits came to me*
> *To make me a shaman . . .*
> *You must follow them*
> *They will make you sick*
> *Until you become a shaman.*
> *If you shake*
> *Then you will get better*
> *All Hmong know that becoming a shaman*
> *Does not come from your will.*

—Paja Thao, "Becoming a Shaman"

The calling is an initiation into the relationships, energies, and powers of the nonordinary worlds. The severe challenge of the calling opens the doors to these worlds and breaks the hold that the ego has on an initiate's perceptions of him- or herself, others, and the world. It forces the initiate to face, engage, and ultimately release inner fears and limitations, while catapulting the initiate into a different dimension of reality and understanding. The calling is a big event in the life of the neophyte shaman that causes a breakdown of the ego, a dismantling of the world as the initiate knew it, and opens the initiate to a new way of perceiving the world and acting in it. With the ego and self-focus out of the way, the veils of limited perception lift, and the initiate can see and access the powers found in the worlds beyond the ordinary. Detailed accounts from shamans describe a profound change that illuminates initiates from within.

The call to shamanism comes in three distinct ways: through a life crisis, through being selected and given powers by shamanic elders, or an undeniable inner calling. Sometimes the call comes as one big event, sometimes it comes as successive events, and sometimes the types of callings overlap. For example, a prospective shaman may experience one or more illnesses over a period of time. This would be considered a life-crisis call. Another potential shaman may experience an illness that is healed by the spirits, and that shaman may also be selected by, and inherit, spirit powers from a family member or an elder shaman. This call would be considered an overlap of a life-crisis call and a selection and gifting of power by an elder.

Shamans who experience life-crisis callings almost always describe themselves as being selected and gifted powers by the spirits. Shamans across cultures talk about the spirits using such things as physical illnesses, injuries, accidents, mental illness, bouts of madness, personal near-death experiences, near-death experiences of a loved one, severe illness or injury of a loved one, death of loved ones or the tribal family, and total life upheaval as ways to unequivocally grab the attention of the initiate.

Health challenges caused by illness, injuries, and accidents—often severe and considered untreatable—are common life-crisis callings. This kind of calling involves a devastating decline in health and often a feeling of imminent death or a near-death experience. Spontaneous or invoked communications with helping spirits and spirit healings that cure the initiate create a profound journey of initiation into the nonordinary worlds. Shamans who have these experiences are referred to as wounded healers. Wounded healers are seen to have healed themselves or been healed by the spirits in miraculous ways not understood by the general populous. These neophytes must then begin shamanic training and enter into service to the people. If they resist the calling, they will likely become ill or injured over and over again until they accept their calling. In the lore of shamanic cultures, anthropological texts, and modern-day accounts, stories of wounded-healer shamans and shamanic practitioners abound. Shamans called by a life crisis tend to

> *The calling is a big event that causes a breakdown of the ego, a dismantling of the world as the initiate knew it, and opens the initiate to a new way of perceiving the world and acting in it.*

be the healthiest when following their spirit calling or soul destiny of being of service to humanity or their community and when staying connected to energy and the spirits.

Psychological crises, mental illnesses, and bouts of madness are, in many cases, signs—and sometimes the hallmark—of a shamanic calling. These experiences are known to open the doors to the non-ordinary, spirit realms of energy and power in quick and extraordinary ways. Like shamans who undergo physical illness and healing as their calling, shamans who experience mental illness or madness are pulled immediately and spontaneously into the realms of spirit to sink or swim, so to speak. In these spontaneous states of ecstasy, neophyte shamans create relationships with helping spirits, begin to connect with energies, and learn the topography of the nonordinary worlds that they will return to in their initiations, training, and work. In many cases, mental illness or bouts of madness are a calling and an initiation combined.

Those called to shamanism by a life crisis tend to be healthiest when they are following their spirit calling or soul destiny of being of service to humanity and their community and when staying connected to energies and the spirits.

The total upheaval of one's life; the near-death experience of a loved one; the severe illness or injury of a loved one; or the death of loved ones, neighbors, or the neophyte's entire community or tribal family are other ways that spirit calls to the unsuspecting shaman-to-be to take up a life of service. The pain and suffering initiates experience from losing or nearly losing everything and everyone that they hold dear, or their close or intimate connections with others, compels the initiates to step onto the shamanic path and learn how to help ease the pain and suffering of the human experience.

Often in these callings of personal crisis or crisis involving a loved one, family, or community, the initiates are able to accomplish feats requiring unusual power without thought for their own health or safety. Figure 14, an illustration from the children's book *The Legend of the Lady's Slipper,* depicts a neophyte shaman rising to meet her challenge. In this story, the shaman Running Flower is spirit-guided to race to a distant village through the deep snow on a dark and

The Hollow Bone

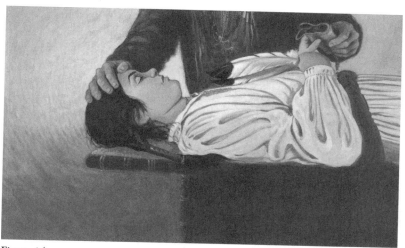

Figure 14

frozen night to obtain medicine to fight a great illness that has overtaken most of her tribe. Empowered by her father's eagle feathers, she returns, exhausted and frozen, to her village, bearing the pouch containing the important medicine.

In some cultures, apprentice shamans receive a call as well as shamanic knowledge, powers, and spirit relationships from shaman elders or shamans within their own families. Benefactors may set up arduous training designed to foster specific achievements or trials and initiations that the apprentice must successfully complete. They may lead an apprentice through specific cultural rites of passage. Benefactors may also transmit knowledge, powers, and spirit relationships to the apprentice at the moment of their death. A shaman who has passed may return to an apprentice in dreams, as might that shaman's helping spirits.

Potential shamans selected by shaman elders are usually (though not always) chosen at a young age, when the elders notice something special or extraordinary about them. Sometimes something special happens during or shortly after their day of birth or the child is heard talking or seen behaving in certain ways that indicate spirit connection or possession. Sometimes the initiate experiences unique, profound visions or dreams or successfully performs healing without training. The initiate might display an undeniable compulsion to learn shamanism at a young age when other children are focused on play or learning to hunt or fight, or an initiate might be able to easily memorize long stories or songs. Elder shamans are always on the watch for individuals showing signs of contact with the spirits.

A powerful description of two types of callings, a life crisis and selection by an elder, comes from Chuonnasuan, the last master shaman among the Tungus people in Siberia. "I had a direct call from the spirits to become a shaman," Chuonnasuan said, adding:

> It is not that anyone can become a shaman if one wants. It is the intention of the spirits that a person becomes a shaman. First I had a direct call from the spirits to become a shaman [his first initiatory illness], and then I learned I could become a shaman when I was in a trance. Then later I was asked to become a shaman when Zhao Li Ben healed me and Zhao's spirits told me I could become a shaman. I was then told of the different roles or powers of the spirits of Zhao, which spirits could cause disease and which could heal.[12]

Agnes Baker-Pilgrim, also known as Grandma Aggie, is a Takelma Indian elder, Confederated Tribes of Siletz. Pictured in Figure 15, she is part of the International Council of Thirteen Indigenous Grandmothers, comprising shamans from around the world who come together through vision and prophecy to form a global alliance of prayer, education, and healing for the earth and for all of its inhabitants and children for the next seven generations. In an article for the magazine *World Pulse*, Grandma Aggie shared this description of her calling:

Elder shamans are always on the watch for individuals showing signs of contact with the spirits.

> I'm the oldest living female left of the Rogue River Indians, who lived in Southern Oregon for over 20,000 years. As a registered member of my tribe, The Confederated Tribes of Siletz Indians, for many, many years I have served on tribal committees always fighting for cultural and traditional improvements. My children and I are all traditional First Nations natives and we "walk our talk." I've been at death's door; I have survived cancer

Figure 15

since 1982. I asked my Creator to let me live because my family needs me and I've got a lot to do. I said, "If you let me live, I'll keep busy the rest of my life." And I'm certainly doing that!

Years ago when I was 45, I experienced a restlessness. This sensation was not only present in my waking hours but also in the dream time. There was a force pulling me toward a spiritual path. I was told to cleanse my inner self. Ultimately, I did what I call a "dying to self." But first I fought this inner-calling, thinking I wasn't worthy to do it. Looking back, however, I can see where I began to change. I started to fly around and I went to all my six children and asked them to forgive me for any hurts I caused them. I asked them to voice anything they wanted to me. I told them how much I loved them and that I would pray for them. I know I made mistakes as a parent.

Yet I still hadn't committed myself to walk this "spiritual" path. I was still arguing to my Creator. Finally one day my friend, who is a psychiatrist, told me to stop fighting this path and resign myself and just do it. So, I did. It was like a big load was lifted off of me.

Handed down from my people was a story that the only duty left to us from the ancient ones was the duty of prayer, so I became a prayer person. The Creator has answered many, many prayers and I give blessings for allowing me to be a mediator.[13]

The most subjective and questioned call to shamanism is the undeniable inner calling. Shamans who experience this type of call often find themselves overtaken by dreams, visions, experiences, signs, messages, and omens that propel them toward the shamanic way of living.

In most shamanic cultures, people try desperately to avoid or escape being called into shamanic service because of the trials, self-sacrifice, constant testing, and demand for self-examination and growth inherent in this way of living and being. But because status and power are inherent in the role of the shaman, it's easy to question the intentions of someone receiving an inner calling to shamanism. Initiates responding to inner callings often undergo more lengthy and extensive training and testing than other shamans. If these shaman initiates are operating with a true spirit calling and connection, they will endure and transcend their training, testing, and inquisitions from the people, their teachers/shaman benefactors, and the spirits, and they will find for themselves that the calling is clear, undeniable, and unquestionable. This type of calling could be seen as a selection by and gift from spirit, or a life-crisis calling, except that

Shamans who receive undeniable inner callings are often propelled to the shamanic way of living by dreams, visions, experiences, signs, messages, and omens.

The Hollow Bone

it comes from within, rather than from without. Life-crisis callings from within typically entail some sort of self-healing or life change that initiates make of their own accord, in connection with the energies and guidance of their helping spirits. Examples might include healing one's self from a chronic physical illness, changing one's attitudes and beliefs toward others or situations in life, or overcoming depression and anxiety by connecting with helping spirits and using shamanic healing techniques.

Training, Initiations, and Rites of Passage

Once you have been confronted with a life-and-death situation, trivia no longer matters. Your perspective grows and you live at a deeper level. There's no time for pettiness. —Margaretta Rockefeller

If, after receiving a calling, the initiate agrees to undertake the path of a shaman, training is the essential next step. Types and lengths of training vary greatly from culture to culture. But shamanic training is always a very personal and individualized process determined by the initiate's spirit guidance; shaman elder(s), teacher(s), or benefactor(s); and the spirit guidance of those teachers.

During training, initiates spend time in nonordinary reality, fortifying their relationships with their helping spirits and learning how to garner energy, power, and wisdom in order to help others.

During training, initiates generally spend a great deal of time in nonordinary reality, fortifying their relationships with their helping spirits and learning how to garner energy, power, and wisdom from the spirits and the nonordinary worlds in order to help others. During this time, they also learn about, make, and gather sacred tools, such as skins, body parts, or representations of their power animals, helping spirits, nature spirits and the elemental spirits; ceremonial clothing; sacred musical instruments, such as drums, rattles, flutes, and bells; and other sacred items. Learning about medicinal plants and plant spirits may also be a part of the training. In some cultures, spirit-given songs are integral to a shaman's work, and an initiate will spend time receiving and learning songs from the spirits and the shaman elders. During training, initiates also learn healing techniques, ceremonial philosophy and procedures, and important tribal wisdom through stories and oral teachings.

Initiations are often an important part of the training process, acting as catalysts for the personal clearing that helps initiates know the self and become clear receptors for spirit energy and communication. Neo-shamans refer to the process of becoming a clear receptor as becoming a hollow bone.

Initiations test and prepare the initiate for the rigors of shamanic service. It can be difficult for a shaman to always be in connection with the pain and suffering of the human experience. Initiations test and prepare one for this connection.

Initiations also test the integrity of the initiate. In some cultures, this testing is paramount, while in others it is less important. Some cultures believe that if the calling didn't kill you, the initiation might. If it doesn't, then you are worthy of serving the community. In these and other cultures, initiations also build rapport between the initiates and their helping spirits and test the strength of the connection between the two.

> *Initiations are catalysts for the personal clearing that helps initiates know the self and become clear receptors for spirit energy and communication. Neo-shamans refer to the process of becoming a clear receptor as becoming a hollow bone.*

Several years ago, I was blessed to take part in a ceremony with Macki Ruka, a Maori Tumula from New Zealand, during one of his peace tours in the United States. After the ceremony, during the time for questions, Macki shared that a Tumula is like a medicine man, only more, doing everything his tribe needs him to do—doctoring, delivering babies, transmuting energies, speaking with the dead, telling stories, keeping ancient wisdom, and activating the vibrations of healing. He began his training as a medicine man at age three, when the Maori Grandmothers chose him to be a shaman. (The Maori are a matriarchal society.) A year or so before he became a qualified medicine man at age nine, the Grandmothers took him, in the middle of the night, by boat, far out into the ocean, beyond the sight of land, and threw him overboard. He described seeing black shapes in the water and feeling scared. Soon the black shapes revealed themselves to be whales. Since by then he could communicate with nature, the whales swam with him and talked to him. They told him to grab on to them and ride them; he did, and they took him deep into the ocean, where the whales exhaled often so he could breathe their air. He had a powerful connection with the whales from that point forward, and he used it with honor and reverence in his work.

Initiations can be both mentor and spirit induced. Mentor-induced initiations vary greatly from culture to culture, and they are sometimes based on the type of calling the initiate received and how the shamans and the culture view this calling. Common mentor-induced initiations include vision quests, use of psychoactive substances or entheogens, and tests of an initiate's commitment and spiritual strength and connections.

Spirit-induced initiations are often recurring or ongoing callings that bring initiates into service and provide them with the staying power they need to continue working for the people; these initiations may include illness, hardship, metaphorical dismemberment in the spirit worlds, or tests of spiritual potency. Other spirit-induced initiations described by shamanic accounts include difficult life situations, handicaps, hardship, illness, injury, loss of loved ones, relationship issues, and loss of spirit connections and healing powers. It is quite common for both new initiates and accomplished shamans to be called by Spirit to undertake trials that either begin or continue to test and train the shaman.

Initiates may undertake vision quests when assigned by mentors, guided by spirit, or compelled by their own initiative. Vision quests are not just a facet of shamanic training; practicing shamans also periodically use them as a tool. In addition to testing initiates, vision quests open the doors to the non-ordinary worlds of spirit. Shamans may undertake them to strengthen spiritual connections, to receive visions and guidance about their role as shaman, or to receive healing, wisdom, and knowledge for the people.

The visions and experiences that occur during a vision quest often change a shaman's way of thinking, increase one's spiritual and healing powers, and provide necessary information for the people the shaman serves.

These quests usually entail sitting alone in the solitude of the wilderness, perhaps at a power place or sacred site, for several or many days and nights without food or water. The profound visions and experiences that occur during a vision quest are known to remarkably change a shaman's way of thinking, increase one's spiritual and healing powers, and often provide necessary information for the people the shaman serves.

Ingesting entheogens is another way that shamans in training shift their consciousness and enter into the nonordinary worlds of spirit. Learning to work with the spirits of psychoactive plants in safe, productive ways takes practice, patience, reverence, knowledge, and gratitude, all developed over time. With training and guidance from the shaman elder, assistance interpreting their experiences, repeated use, and a gradual increase in the amount of the plant they use, initiates build a relationship with these powerful plants and plant spirits and are able to use them to augment their healing practice.

Tests of commitment and spiritual strength and connections involve seemingly unattainable tasks, such as arduous travel to sacred sites, long runs through the desert with no water, mountain climbing, fording raging rivers, walking across hot coals, piercings, brandings, bee stings, ant stings, walking through a nest of snakes, diving from high cliffs, or spending the night alone in known predator-animal territories with animal blood smeared on one's body to invite the animal in. These tests vary widely and depend on an initiate's location, culture, training norms, and the shaman elder's spirit guidance. Enduring pain, both physical and emotional, pushes initiates to the edges of stamina, fortitude, and sanity, not only testing their commitment, but also hurling them into deeper connection with their helping spirits and the energies of the nonordinary worlds. As initiates accomplish the tasks of the test, they gain power from the spirits involved, such as the spirit of the sacred place, river, mountain, bees, or predatory animal. The more spirit allies that initiates develop, the greater the power that initiates have to heal and help the people.

As initiates accomplish the tasks of the test, they gain power from the spirits involved. And the more spirit allies initiates develop, the greater the initiates' power to heal and help will be.

The Hollow Bone

Dismemberment is a common initiation brought about by spirit when the initiate or shaman is in nonordinary reality. Dismemberments facilitate a shamanic death for the purpose of healing; while in the spirit worlds, the shaman typically experiences a metaphorical physical dismemberment and death, while his or her actual, physical body, present in the ordinary world, experiences no pain or discomfort. Once "bodyless," the shaman experiences what it is like to be spirit energy, free of the confines of the physical body. Before the shaman returns to ordinary reality, the body is reassembled, or "remembered," minus debilitating energy intrusions and blockages. The dismemberment/shamanic death releases the stronghold of the "old mind," stimulating new ways of thinking and a new awareness of the spirit-self's connection to the web of life.

An initiate is ready to begin practicing healing and other shamanic services when:

- A shaman elder determines he or she is ready and holds a ceremony announcing the rite of passage

- An initiate's teacher considers the initiate competent in skills and ready to practice

- The initiate feels competent in skills and guided to practice

- Spirit guides the initiate to begin to practice, no matter what the initiate's stage of training

- Successful healings occur as a direct result of the initiate's practice

- A life crisis occurs

Sometimes when an initiate's training is lengthy or simply taking longer than spirit is willing to wait, a life crisis will occur to prompt the initiate into service. Such was the case with Chuonnasuan, the last master shaman among the Tungus peoples, quoted earlier. He had three illnesses that initiated him first into training and then into practice.

The shaman's path is unending. I am an old, old man and still a baby, standing before the mystery of the world, filled with awe.
—Don José Matsuwa, Huichol shaman, quoted in **Shamanic Voices** by Joan Halifax

Part Three

Shamanic
Practices

Chapter 6

The Foundation
of Shamanic Practice

A first definition of this complex phenomenon, and perhaps the least hazardous, will be: shamanism = technique of ecstasy.

Mircea Eliade, *Shamanism: Archaic Techniques of Ecstasy*

Anyone who studies shamanism for very long will soon recognize that there are several principles consistent throughout shamanic cultures. There is no doctrine, and there are no rules for shamanism, so these principles are not dictated or carved in stone. Instead, they are ways of thinking and acting that serve both the shamans and the people.

The survival of the shaman's people is, to a large extent, placed on the shoulders of the shaman. Therefore, shamans cannot afford to be indolent, muddled in their own issues, or using their power inefficiently or frivolously. It is believed that if shamans are not clear of mind, focused on the intention of their work, working for the good of the people, constantly honing their skills, and honoring their relationships with nature and the spirits, they lose their power. Out of the mother of necessity grows the shamanic principles of awareness, impeccability, practicality, gratitude, and freedom of spirit.

Awareness

Shamans know that energy and power are key elements to their work on behalf of the people. They know that everything is living and, therefore, is energy. When shamans perform a ceremony or help a person heal, they deal directly with the omnipresent necessary energies. They know that everything speaks messages to them and that by being fully aware and paying close attention to all of the signs, omens, and portents, they can read what is happening in their world and garner energy and power to help the people when needed. They do so with the utmost economy of energy and with gratitude. Life is sacred, and shamans honor it, never forgetting the value of life, soul, nature, and spirit.

Shamans know that to be of service, they must maintain a clear mind, focused intention, and relationships with helping spirits.

Shamans know that in order to be of service, they must maintain both a clear mind and focused intention. Intention is the goal, purpose, or meaning of an action or a practice. Intent binds shamans to the task, focuses their energy to that task, enables their helping spirits to effectively empower and interact with them, and helps them understand and clearly interpret the experience.

Earth teach me quiet—
as the grasses are still with new light.

Earth teach me suffering—
as old stones suffer with memory.

Earth teach me humility—
as blossoms are humble with beginning.

Earth teach me caring—
as mothers nurture their young.

Earth teach me courage—
as the tree that stands alone.

Earth teach me limitation—
as the ant that crawls on the ground.

Earth teach me freedom—
as the eagle that soars in the sky.

Earth teach me acceptance—
as the leaves that die each fall.
Earth teach me renewal—
as the seed that rises in the spring.

Earth teach me to forget myself—
as melted snow forgets its life.

Earth teach me to remember kindness—
as dry fields weep with rain.

—Ute prayer

Impeccability

The shaman's connection with spirit requires intense dedication, focus, intention, and clarity. Maintaining these qualities requires that shamans pay close attention to themselves and live impeccably.

Shamanic impeccability is not about right and wrong. It is about each individual shaman living according to his or her energetic nature and spirit guidance and from his or her own soul and spirit connections. Because the soul is not muddled or tainted by individual or cultural bias, opinion, or judgment, working from the soul allows shamans to maintain clarity.

Living impeccably is not about being a model member of the tribe or community; it is about being internally consistent within oneself. Shamans understand that when they or

Living impeccably means being internally consistent with oneself, being true to the natural self.

someone in the community does something that is not true to their natural self, they will leak energy, lose personal power, and form energy blockages that may be experienced as emotional discomfort or a decline in physical health. In the shaman's point of view, doing something not consistent with one's natural self is neither a practical nor an efficient use of energy.

Practicality

Shamanism has grown out of the potent need for someone to understand and apply both the knowledge of human behavior and the wisdom and energies of the elements, nature, and spirits to ensure the survival and health of the people. It is a path of absolute practicality and ingenuity. The only thing that matters is what works right here, right now, for the client, village, or intention, in any given situation. Because shamanism is a path of direct revelation, no two practices or situations are the same, even when the same shaman works with the same helping spirits on behalf of the same client. Every situation is different; the shaman is always in connection with the changing circumstances and energies and is focused on the practicality of what will work and what needs to happen at any given moment.

> *Shamanism is a path of absolute practicality and ingenuity. The only thing that matters is what works right here, right now, for the client, village, or intention, in any given situation.*

In Figure 16, we can see a demonstration of this practicality and ingenuity. Ecuadorian shaman Don Esteban Tamayo, an Otavalean Quichua Indian who lives in Carabuela, near Otavalo; his wife, Mama Rosita; and his grandson, Esteban Jr. (a shaman apprentice), use palm leaves, candles, carnation petals, sacred stones (*huacas*), bottles of sugar-cane schnapps (*trago*), cologne water, cinnamon, and *Ishpingo* dust to perform a cleaning and healing for a sick Canadian client. The person could not be present, so the shamans are using a photo and clothes, brought by a friend, to represent the person and to act as an energy conduit for the work being performed. The clothes and photo bring the energy of the ill person to the shamans in Ecuador; because energy travels freely and immediately, the client starts to receive the energies and benefits as soon as the shamanic healing work begins. The client will continue to receive these energies throughout the friend's trip and when the clothes and photo are returned. Here we see the practicality and flexibility of the shaman, who does what needs to be done in this situation to overcome what others might perceive as a barrier or a limitation.

Figure 16

Gratitude

Shamans are able to do what works best and most efficiently in any situation because of their extensive training and because of the direct guidance from their helping spirits. So shamans know they must maintain their powerful relationships with the helping spirits. They never forget that their power to help others comes from their helping spirits and from the energies of nature and the many worlds. They believe that if they do not honor whom and where their power comes from, their power will leave them.

Freedom of Spirit

Shamans know that their function is to be a clear connection to the compassionate helping spirits and the nonordinary worlds. They know they are to obtain power and wisdom from these worlds, and that they are to act as a buffering force for the chaotic energies impacting the people. Shamans do all of these things by cultivating and harnessing self-power that is fueled and guided by their spirit allies. Shamans must remain uninfluenced by the opinions, behaviors, or practices of others while being astutely observant. They must participate in and remain open to the human experience, yet stay detached from it.

Differences in cultural traditions, values, and belief systems mean nothing to shamans. The spirit levels they inhabit and the energies they connect with are far beyond the scope of the limited human mind, which believes the illusion that the spiritual world and physical worlds are separate. While shamans live in and may teach and mirror the myths and traditions of their culture, they are by no means ruled by their culture. Shamans are essentially free spirits that come and go in their quest to connect with the boundless, most pure forms of life-force, nature, and spirit energies.

As I walk, as I walk
The universe is walking with me
In beauty it walks before me
In beauty it walks behind me
In beauty it walks below me
In beauty it walks above me
Beauty is on every side
As I walk, I walk with Beauty.

—Traditional Navajo prayer

Chapter 7

Practices from
Around the World

*When we can look at a tree and say, "There is life," and when we can
look at a rock or a cloud and say, "There is life," then we can look
within ourselves and find respect for all life. Then we can see the true
nature of our relationship with the world and better comprehend the
need to exist in harmony with the earth. Then rain will fall when it
is needed, and sun will shine on a beautiful and viable world.*

Nan Moss and David Corbin, *Weather Shamanism*

In this chapter, we'll look at common shamanic practices found in
many diverse cultures around the world. Shamans help people heal
and serve people, nature, and the earth by entering the nonordinary
worlds of spirit and traversing a specific cosmology, by honing their
senses, by becoming a hollow bone, by entering into trance (also
known as shamanic journeying), by performing ceremonies, by telling stories of wisdom and healing, by tapping into specific rhythms
by singing sacred songs, by harnessing energy, and by using sacred
tools and the art of omenology to garner energy and wisdom from
all of the worlds.

Shamans commonly enter into trance to travel into, connect with, and traverse the energies and landscapes of the nonordinary worlds of spirit. First, we will explore the nonordinary-world cosmologies. Then we will explore the techniques shamans use to enter into and work with these worlds and the powerful life force energies found there.

Entering and Exploring Nonordinary-World Cosmologies

[T]he image of the tree represents a template for the structure of reality, and the emergence of multiplicity (branches, twigs and leaves) out of unity (the trunk), of the visible (the tree above ground) out of the invisible, (the hidden part of the tree—the roots below ground). —M. Alan Kazlev

Shamans throughout the world know that the nonordinary worlds of spirit, sometimes referred to as the otherworld(s) or spirit realms, consist of three unique divisions, or cosmologies or worlds, of energy and reality. The powers and the mysteries of these worlds keep shamans exploring throughout their entire life.

To enter into the nonordinary worlds of spirit, the shaman or shamanic practitioner passes through a portal or gateway to gain entrance to what is called the central axis. The central axis isn't a place, but is instead sacred energy that functions as the center of all the worlds and links the worlds together. It passes through every dimension and has openings into all of the otherworlds. The central axis acts like a vacuum, an express tram, or an elevator transporting the shaman and shamanic practitioner to the otherworld entrances. Representations of the central axis vary across cultures, but all descriptions are similar. The central axis is commonly symbolized as a center pole or sacred pillar that can be ascended and descended, entered and exited at any point. It is

> *To enter into the nonordinary worlds of spirit, shamans pass through a portal or gateway to enter what is called the central axis. The central axis isn't a place, but is instead sacred energy that functions as the center of all the worlds and links the worlds together.*

The Hollow Bone

known by such names as the Tree of Life, the World Tree, the Golden Pillar, the Middle Pillar, the World Pillar, and the Celestial Column. The Cosmic Mountain is another common representation of the central axis. Castles, churches, temples, and pyramids have been built as replicas to honor and capture this energy.

Figure 17 shows a drawing of a Tree of Life. In many cultures, the Tree of Life represents not only the central axis of the spirit worlds

Figure 17

but also shamans themselves. It symbolizes how the shaman is a rooted, living channel between earth and sky, a bridge between the people and spirit. This ancient symbol can be found in nearly every culture and religion.

Most shamanic cultures view the universe as having three levels: earth, underworld, and sky. In core-shamanism, as presented by Dr. Michael Harner and the Foundation for Shamanic Studies, these levels are referred to as the middle world, lower world, and upper world. Where the shaman goes depends on the shaman's intention, the client's needs or the service that is being carried out, and the guidance of the shaman's helping spirits.

All three worlds have multiple layers or levels within them. The ability to discern these sublevels and which sublevels a shaman sees depends on that particular shaman and his or her helping spirits.

Most shamanic cultures view the universe as having three levels: earth, underworld, and sky. In core-shamanism, these levels are referred to as the middle, lower, and upper worlds.

The middle world, or earth, is the world we live in. It has both physical and spiritual aspects that overlap and interplay. The upper world, or sky, and the lower world, or underworld, are places of spiritual power and high-vibrational energies that do not have physical aspects. At times, the images that shamans experience in the upper and lower worlds may appear physical, because that is how the human psyche interprets the energies of spirit and the otherworlds. (It bears noting that these worlds have nothing to do with religious delineations, such as heaven or hell, as shamanism has been in existence long before Christianity came into existence.)

Helping spirits reside in all of the worlds. Shamans must access these worlds in order to connect with the energies and spirits inherent there. They can use these energies and spirits for many things, including empowering themselves; gaining spiritual strength; obtaining spiritual guidance, wisdom, knowledge, or new innovations; or accessing ongoing assistance with healing techniques or garnering and applying healing energy.

Because each shaman is unique, the terrain of the worlds in which he or she travels is also unique, unless the shaman has been trained to travel to culturally specific places in the nonordinary worlds. The worlds hold infinite landscapes, colors, smells, tastes, sensations, energies, powers, medicines, helping spirits, and experiences.

The following three paragraphs describe some of the aspects of the three worlds found in common throughout shamanic cultures. Remember, there are no absolute descriptions; even though shamans spend a great deal of time in the nonordinary worlds of spirit, exploring and attempting to comprehend them, no one can tell you what *you* might experience in any of these worlds. But some generalities are consistent from account to account and from culture to culture.

The lower world is frequently depicted as earthy and primal, with the topography and landscape similar to those of places on the earth. Some shamans experience images and sensations that give them the feeling of being in the earth, such as in a cave or cavern. It is often experienced as being elemental; individual elements and combinations of earth, air, fire, and water often lend their energies to the intention of the shaman visiting the lower world. It is common to meet many power animals in the lower world, though helping spirits of all kinds are described as being found here. Many shamanic traditions believe that the lower world is the womb of Mother Earth. Shamans commonly ask to enter the lower world for healing of all types, for self and others, as well as many other reasons.

The middle world, the world of the people's everyday life, has both physical and spiritual aspects. It is where the ordinary and nonordinary worlds overlap.

The upper world is generally described as appearing airy and ethereal; it is composed of a high-vibrational energy that may leave the shaman feeling lightheaded. Sparkling lights, velvety blackness, bright white light, rainbow swirls, clouds, crystal temples, mountains, pyramids, pulsating energy patterns, symbols, cosmic matter, and pastel or vibrant colors are common in upper-world accounts. These accounts frequently describe helping spirits in human form and include descriptions of shamans connecting with deceased ancestors, loved ones, and ascended masters. Power animals also appear in upper-world accounts, as do mythical beings. Shamans often ask to enter the upper world to receive high-vibrational energy cleansing, power-filling, healing, guidance, wisdom, and teachings for themselves and on behalf of the client and community.

The middle world is the world of the people's everyday life, having both physical and spiritual aspects. It is where the ordinary and non-ordinary worlds overlap. It is a parallel, yet inclusive, universe of infinite, coexisting energies, unlimited by space and time. It is the world of balance and integration of perceptual dual opposites, like joy and suffering, pain and passion, light and dark, good and bad, science and spirituality, male and female, empowering and power-draining influences. The middle world is the place where energy vibrates at its slowest rate. Here, energy can become stagnant and cause illness and despair, or it can flow freely, creating health and joy. Shamans often enter the nonordinary realms of the middle world to visit locations and to check in on people and situations they can't travel to or see in ordinary, physical reality; they might also enter the middle world's spiritual realms to access life-force and nature-spirit energies, to locate lost power or objects, or to divine and seek guidance for tribal and community ceremonies, activities, and moves.

Honing the Senses

I begin with the initiation of the heart. I try to stop the "mind chatter." This is different than meditation which lasts for a short time then you process and go back to your normal life. I give them the gift of finding things that people take with them every second, every minute, every hour, every day of their lives. They carry the love and become the teacher. They teach themselves and bring it to others. —Macki Ruka, a Maori Tumula

Extraordinary awareness of the universe is the shaman's gift, and maintaining it is the shaman's responsibility. The body, senses, thoughts, feelings, emotions, energy field, and spirit of the shaman are all tuned to pick up even the slightest detail that can tell the shaman the actuality of any given situation.

Shamans learn early in their training, usually as early as their calling, that unwavering honesty helps them see and understand the worlds and the people they serve. Unwavering honesty is much more than simply telling the truth. It requires that shamans not only observe what most people see, but also see it with shaman eyes—to see it *as it actually is,* not as other people perceive it, want it to be, or think it should be. Shamans see what actually is by observing everything with a fully open, unattached mind; by paying attention to every detail; and by looking through the eyes of their helping spirits.

In their training, shamans spend a good deal of time learning how to hone their observation senses and learning how to "see" with their whole body. The ability to "see in the dark" is the ability to see into the nonordinary worlds of spirit and to see and experience things in the ordinary world that most people miss. Their teacher(s) and helping spirits train shamans to relax the mind and body, to consciously silence mind chatter, and to drop any preconceived notions about what they are observing. Sometimes long periods in seclusion and trance are used to fine-tune the shaman's instruments of perception. Many stories describe how shamans:

> *Shamans not only observe what most people see, but also see it as it actually is—not as other people perceive it, want it to be, or think it should be.*

- Set their intention

- Desire to see clearly

- Focus by mindfully directing their attention to what they are observing

- Release their place in the world by stopping mind chatter and everyday worldly thoughts, allowing themselves to be fully present in the experience

- Become aware of, and receptive to, all of the feelings, sensations, and insights that come to them

- Accept what comes without judgment or analytical censoring

In this state of mindful, bare awareness, shamans access one of the most potent faculties humans have for perceiving energy and spirit— their *felt sense*. The felt sense is the combination of all of the feelings, sensations, and realizations that the shaman experiences at any given time, from multiple sensations to spirit information. Remarkably, shamans are simultaneously conscious and aware of everything they are feeling in their physical body, everything they are thinking and feeling emotionally, what is happening with them energetically, what they are sensing intuitively, what is happening around them, and the spirit interaction with all of these sensations. Shamans take in the whole, unedited picture whenever they use the felt sense.

Becoming as balanced, calm, clear, and whole within themselves as possible helps shamans become a clear channel for spiritual energies and correctly interpret the wisdom found in these energies.

By exploring and utilizing all of the senses, including and extending out beyond just the five physical senses, shamans discern the forces that drive not only the universe, but also the individual sentient beings that live within it. Shamans begin by exploring and understanding the layers of the self. The circular nature of life shows shamans that their spirits are eternal, even while their bodies are ephemeral. Just as energy cannot be created or destroyed, neither can the spirit nor soul of a person. If the body is temporary and the spirit is eternal, then the spirit must have a reason, an agenda, for occupying a human body.

During their calling, shamans discover that the agenda for them is to heal and to be of service to the people by becoming an instrument of communication between the nonordinary worlds of spirit and the ordinary world. In order to be a clear channel for spiritual communication and energies, shamans must do the challenging work of clearing away attachments, detrimental and limiting behaviors, unhealthy mind-sets, and energetic blockages and intrusions. This clearing occurs during their training and initiations and continues throughout their life. This integration of body, mind, emotion, energy field, and spirit allows the shaman to be a hollow bone, through which spirit can express itself clearly and cleanly.

Becoming a Hollow Bone

Divinity has one ultimate secret, which it will also whisper in your ear if your mind becomes quieter than the fog at sunset: the God of this world is found within, and you know it is found within: in those hushed silent times when the mind becomes still, the body relaxes into infinity, the senses expand to become one with the world—in those glistening times, a subtle luminosity, a serene radiance, a brilliantly transparent clarity shimmers as the true nature of all manifestation, erupting every now and then in a compassionate Radiance before whom all idols retreat, a love so fierce it adoringly embraces both light and dark, both good and evil, both pleasure and pain equally. —Ken Wilber, "The Destruction of the World Trade Center"

Shamans operate knowing that there is no one way to do things. What works is what matters. Therefore, the shaman relies on many different tools and techniques and on spirit guidance to know and perform what is necessary at any given time. A community's survival often depended on this understanding. If the shaman's information about the weather, a hunt, or an illness was incorrect or misinterpreted, people suffered and perhaps died. If the information was correct and the shaman clearly interpreted it, they flourished.

Shamans know that to be capable of entering the nonordinary worlds, they must become the hollow bone. Becoming as balanced, calm, clear, and whole within themselves as possible helps them become a clear channel for the energies and correctly interpret the wisdom found in these energies, to effectively help themselves and others. Shamans constantly use vigilant, bare awareness to look within themselves and to clear away thoughts, emotions, behaviors, and energetic debris that can clog and diminish their abilities. This awareness, both internal and external, is vitally important to the shaman. Shamans pay attention to all dreams, both night dreams and daydreams, and know that all life experiences, all relationships, and the helping spirits work in partnership with them to facilitate this hollowing process.

Seeing consistent, effective results from a shaman's work indicates that shaman has successfully become a hollow bone for channeling spiritual energy.

The world is a manifestation of the web of life and is, in itself, an intelligent being that communicates with us in every moment. Shamans know that these subtle messages provide key information and insights into one's self and the world. By paying close attention to life, to the signs, messages, and omens that come into their world in myriad ways, shamans can continually check how clear the channel is and how well spiritual energy is flowing. If the shaman and the people see consistent, effective results from the shaman's healing and service work, that shaman is clearly able to be a hollow bone with clear spirit and energy connections.

Entering into Trance, or Shamanic Journeying

The first meditators in history were the shamans, whose practices for contemplation and connecting with the divine are echoed in virtually every spiritual tradition today. —Sandra Ingerman, *Shamanic Meditations*

Shamanic journeying is an ancient practice common to all indigenous societies. Entering into trance is to make an ecstatic shift of consciousness that is measurable by brain-wave frequencies. Also called dreaming, journeying, the shamanic state of consciousness, ecstasy, and madness, trance is the way the shaman or shamanic practitioner enters the alpha, theta, or delta brain-wave frequencies. The trance state used by many shamans and journeyers is the theta state of brain-wave activity, the state that is the closest to sleep and the deepest conscious state most people can sustain. Many shamans are called dreamers or are said to be "dreaming" the journey. This state feels similar to daydreaming, though it is much, much deeper.

Entering into trance, or shamanic journeying, is also referred to as dreaming, the shamanic state of consciousness, ecstasy, and madness.

Shifting into a shamanic state of consciousness allows shamans to move their awareness beyond the ordinary world, sinking beneath the analytical, conscious, critical, left-brained mind. In this state of deep awareness, shamans can connect with and explore the realms of vast possibility in the nonordinary worlds of spirit, energies, and helping spirits.

Shamans enter into trance with the assistance of monotonous, rhythmic drumming or other percussion, rattling, dancing, chanting, singing, nonlyrical music, movement, verbal narration, specific breathing technologies, or entheogens. Figure 18 shows the late Pau Karma Wangchuk, a Tibetan shaman, dancing to enter a trance state during a ceremony.

Once the journeyer enters this trance state of consciousness, the journey begins. Journeying is natural like dreaming, and everyone can journey. (It is generally accepted that all humans have the ability to journey and learn from their spirit self and their helping spirits.) However, journeying uses certain skills that are not common in modern or nonspiritual societies. Relaxation, imagination, focused intention, concentration, and surrender are skills that the shaman practices to perfection. Relaxation and a quiet mind allow the shaman or journeyer to move from the ordinary world into the nonordinary worlds of spirit. Imagination is the mind power that begins the journey and opens the portals between the ordinary world and the nonordinary worlds. Focused intention and concentration are the energies that move the shaman's imagination forward and into connection with the web. Surrender allows the shaman to go into the experience of the journey without being attached to the outcome; during a journey, shamans give up the ego self, thus giving themselves over to their spirit self and to the experience. Loosening the tight grip that humans hold on their minds, bodies, and perceptions of the world, easing the need to be in control, is a respite for the mind and body.

Figure 18

The images and sensations that shamans experience during their journeys are the language that helping spirits use to communicate with humans.

Shamanic journeying was the first tool of shamanism I learned, and it is a profound healing technique that I use daily. Every journey is a coming home, a resting place, a respite, a sigh of relief, an entry into peace that reconnects me with my helping spirits, inner healer, soul-self, and the divine. Peace, understanding, and calmness permeate my everyday life from this connection of my soul-self with spirit.

Journeying uses certain skills that are not common in modern or nonspiritual societies: relaxation, imagination, focused intention, concentration, and surrender.

Every journey is unique. The following description of one of my journeys is an example of a shaman being deeply engaged and connected with helping spirits, the web, and life-force energies in nature. All journeys are unique and vary from person to person and journey to journey, so this journey should not be assumed to be the norm. It is simply one example of infinite possibilities.

The golden rays of the new morning sun peek around the mountaintops, casting a ghostly glow through the thick lake fog. Within minutes, the misty sunbeams lengthen across the lake, changing the nightly black dress of the surrounding pines into their daytime green. As if signaled by the impending sunrise, the loon who has been fishing quietly next to my canoe extends his neck and sends his eerie call out into the solitude. Shivers run down my spine, and my heart aches with a deep soul connection with this beautiful being and place. My eyes follow his call as it is reverberating over the lake, sliding up the mountains, circling around, and echoing back down. As if heralded by the call, the sun ascends the mountain summit and makes his grand entrance into the day. The brilliance blinds my eyes, and I reluctantly turn away, just in time to catch a glimpse of a soaring silhouette gliding through the golden wisps of fog.

A moment later, our new arrival identifies herself as a loon with her mystical call. Still close to my canoe, her mate answers, and she splashes down next to us. As the ripples of the spring-fed lake calm, she rises up and appears to be dancing to fluff and dry her wings. The two talk in a laughing, chattering dialect, and I am thrilled to bear witness to their interplay. Settling in, the fishing partners go about their work, searching the crystal waters for their shiny breakfasts. The morning grows deeper into day, and the breeze that whispers through the pines kicks up a gentle ripple on the clear waters. Soaring high above the mountaintop, the hawk cries, drawing my attention upward to watch her embrace the new day. A low grunting sound moves up the river behind me toward the lake. The source soon reveals itself as a great blue heron soars in, extends its landing gear, and comes to rest on the beaver lodge. The beaver, gathering leafy twigs nearby, doesn't seem to mind the visitor and continues to go about his work.

An incredible supernatural energy moves in my body as I sit in divine connection with these spirited beings and this pristine wilderness. In awe, my body and soul fill with reverent wonder. I feel whole, peaceful, healthy, and vital, here in the quiet solitude of the wilderness where the song of the universe sings in my soul. Surrounded by this incredible life force, my heart fills with gratitude, and I thank the Spirits and the Creator for blessing me with this opportunity. By allowing myself to sit quietly and "just be," I have given myself a gift of healing beyond measure.

From a distance, the changing drumbeat signals my callback, and I return back into my body, in my healing room at my home. I am reluctant to leave this healing, soul-fulfilling place, but I am thankful to have learned methods that allow me to visit often. Upon returning from my journey, I take a few minutes to journal, feel my body, and integrate my experience. Powerful energy and a deep sense of well-being flow through me.

Journeying is healing on many levels. A strong, healthy body is but one of the many rewards I reap. It is an honor to work with the sacred spirits who are eager to help me live life to the fullest, explore the other worlds, query deep into my inner self, and connect with the divine. Important, hard-to-see truths are revealed during my trips to the otherworlds, and illusions and masks removed. I am able to see myself for who I truly am, not the identities I think I am in this ordinary world. The high-vibrational energy flow of the otherworlds weaves the energies of my spirit soul-self with my body, mind, and emotions so that I can live integrated, balanced, whole, and filled with the life force. Cognitively, it can be difficult to comprehend the healing that I receive through journeying, but feeling the energy that flows into my body and soul is pure ecstasy. My body shakes with energy essence, and my spirit soars free and unencumbered. That experience is undeniable, immeasurable, and it illuminates my everyday living as a healer, teacher, author, mother, wife, athlete, and nature lover.

Stories are real, living, animate beings— energies that live in both the ordinary and nonordinary worlds and move through people to be shared.

Performing Ceremonies

The Creator wants us to drum. He wants us to corrupt the world with drum, dance and chants. After all, we have already corrupted the world with power and greed . . . which hasn't gotten us anywhere—now's the time to corrupt the world with drum, dance and chants. —Babatunde Olatunji

Ceremonies celebrate life and death. Ceremonies celebrate power and energy. Ceremonies celebrate rites of passage. Ceremonies celebrate people, spirit, nature, life-force energies, and the connections of these valuable things in the lives of the people. Ceremonies bring the people together in harmony and purpose. Ceremonies manifest the web in tangible ways that connect the shaman and the people to the greater whole. Ceremonies are seen as gifts from the spirits to the people, to help the people and the shamans connect deeply with spirit and one another. These gifts are sacred, abundant, and freely given. Ceremonies are also offerings of reverence and gratitude from the shaman and the people to the helping spirits and energies of nature whose guidance and powers are essential to the survival and health of the people.

Ceremonies are celebratory not only because of the events that may be the reason for them, but also because being in ceremony opens the shaman and the people to portals provided by spirit. Being in ceremony creates an opportunity for people to shed the everyday world and open their souls to a direct connection with the energies and powers of the nonordinary spirit worlds and the web of life. Like journeying (which is a form of ceremony and sometimes a component of ceremonies), ceremonies open the doors to the sacred and heighten the shaman's and the people's perceptions, so they are able to see, sense, feel, experience, and harness the energies and powers found in the nonordinary worlds of spirit.

Shamans, cocreating with their helping spirits, often facilitate ceremonies. Every ceremony has an intention; as shamans and the people prepare for, perform, and complete the ceremony, they understand the goal and clearly know the meaning of the ceremony. In order for the people and the shaman to effectively use the energies that the ceremony invokes, it is essential that the intention behind it is clear. Maintaining clarity of intention is a job that often falls to the facilitating shaman.

Storytelling

Myths are the guides for the individual disengaging from the social order for an experience of the divine, which is the underlying unity. —Joseph Campbell, quoted in "A Five-Element Analysis of the Grail Myth," by Marcia A. Liberatore, MD

A Grandfather was talking to his grandson about how he felt. He said, "I feel as if I have two wolves fighting in my heart. One wolf is the vengeful, angry, violent one. The other is the loving, compassionate one." The grandson asked him, "Which wolf will win the fight in your heart?" The Grandfather answered, "The one I feed."[14]

Stories are real, living, animate beings. These beings are energies that live in both the ordinary and nonordinary worlds and move through people to be shared. Many stories come from the spirits, and each spirit that a shaman works with may require a forum in which to share its story. Likewise, many stories live with the shaman's people and are passed down in a more rote or formal manner, especially in oral traditions. In each case, stories are alive and dynamic, and all who listen to them can receive their radiant energy, if they are perceptive enough to receive it.

Storytelling is an invaluable practice in both shamanic culture and all of humanity. Storytelling is an art and an honor. Storytelling keeps a culture and its practices alive. It engages the people in their beliefs and traditions, reminding members and teaching both children and new people about the societal history and norms. Regardless of whether the stories are shared by oral tradition, books, or compact-disc recordings, a great share of humanity's wisdom and philosophies have been passed down from generation to generation through stories.

Storytelling is poetic and beautiful, heartbreaking and dreadful. Storytelling is theater at its roots and perhaps also theater's finest expression. Storytelling is tragic, comedic, sensual, thought provoking, emotionally moving, and spiritually engaging. Storytellers may or may not be shamans. If storytellers use spirit connection and guidance in their presentation, then it is likely they are shamanic storytellers, or shamans who use storytelling as one of the tools in their practice.

Throughout history, shamans have used stories, sometimes in clear-cut forms and sometimes in vague parables and riddles, to teach and prepare their apprentices. These stories are specifically designed to help open the apprentices' eyes and mind to see and read energies; notice and understand typically unnoticed occurrences and details; and perceive the human thought, emotional, and energetic patterns of their clients, communities, and enemies. Stories are also crafted to illuminate spirit signs, omens, and messages as they appear in the ordinary and nonordinary worlds. Joseph Campbell, renowned researcher and master of mythology and shamanic culture, tells us that mystics have been taught the cultural and mythological symbols that guide their experience.[15] The phrase "the psychotic will drown in the waters that the mystic swims in because the mystic is readied for what he encounters" is of profound relevance to the shaman, shamanic apprentice, and shamanic practitioner; readying students for mystical waters is the underlying motive of shamans who use stories to teach.

> *If storytellers use spirit connection and guidance in their presentation, then it is likely they are shamanic storytellers.*

A shamanic storyteller uses stories with clients and the community for specific purposes—purposes that are generally multilayered and not always noticeable. For example, a shaman may use a story to share a specific message or to teach a particular learning, while also using it as a tool to focus the listeners' attention and to weave specific energies that help listeners access, open to, and travel through the doors to the nonordinary worlds of spirit. Such a story is often a critically important part of a healing ceremony or session because it prepares and fully engages listeners in the coming healing or spiritual intervention.

These stories were the libraries of our people. In each story, there was recorded some event of interest or importance. . . . A people enrich their minds who keep their history on the leaves of memory.
—Luther Standing Bear, Lakota of the Oglala tribe

Singing Sacred Songs

The Cold offered me
Lays out there
The Rain sent me often Songs
Other Ballads the Wind brought me
The Waves carried them to the Shore
Birds shaped Words into Tones
Talking sounded from the Crowns of Trees.

—From the Kalevala, a Finnish song cycle

The verse above is one of the first in Finland's great song cycle known as the Kalevala. It expresses beautifully the shamanic view that power lives in nature and that nature willingly gives its magic songs to those who will give them voice.

Singing, toning, chanting, whistling, reciting mantras, and singing through an instrument such as a flute or drum are essential features of shamanic practice around the globe. Just like shamanism itself, music and songs related to shamanism and used as a part of it are as diverse as the people, cultures, beliefs, and customs that they live in.

Like stories, songs are real, living, animate beings. These beings are energies that live in both the ordinary and nonordinary worlds and move through people to be shared. Magic or power songs come from the spirits, and each spirit that works with a shaman may call for a forum in which to share its song. It's not unusual for stories to come to the shaman in the form of a song.

Songs are often integral parts of ceremonies and healing practices. Likewise, many songs live with the people and are often passed down in a prescribed manner, especially in oral traditions. In each case, the song is alive and dynamic; each person who shares the song and each person who hears it receives the animated energy, if they are perceptive enough to receive it.

Singing, toning, chanting, whistling, reciting mantras, and singing through an instrument such as a flute or drum are essential features of shamanic practice around the globe.

Shamanic power songs are not composed or created by the song carrier. Shamanic songs may be traditional ceremonial or healing songs that shaman elders teach initiates, or spirits may spontaneously communicate songs to a shaman during journeys, trainings, initiations, quests, ceremonies, and healing experiences. In many instances, power songs simply show up in the head, heart, and soul of the shaman. The songs ferment, bubble up, open out, and burst from the shaman when they can no longer be contained. Sometimes songs have words; sometimes they have just tones, vowel sounds, or nature sounds; sometimes they have just rhythms; and sometimes they have all three.

Many shamanic cultures believe that songs may visit a shaman and stay as long they like or for as long as they are being used. Sometimes they stay for just one use; sometimes they stay for a long time.

Shamans know that power songs come from a source that is magnificent, vast, and powerful, and they feel honored to have been given or visited by such songs. These power or magic songs are spirit inspired and inspirational to the shaman. Shamans delight in the powerful flow of song moving in them. When they feel a song rising, they let go and let the song sing them, play with them, shift them, and change them, all the while witnessing the changes in their body, energy, voice, and breathing as spirit takes over. Many power songs are born out of an ecstatic experience and may be used to induce ecstatic experiences.

Each song has a purpose that the spirits and the shaman are aware of and use in specific ways. Shamans sing for many, many different reasons. Shamans sing open the doors to the nonordinary worlds of spirit and to sing out to call their helping spirits to them. Songs draw in the attention, focus the intention, and weave the energies of the people and the universe together. Songs help one to gently slip out of the ego self and to relax the need for control and convention, so that the powers of nature and the nonordinary worlds can flow through the person unrestricted.

Shamans sing songs in gratitude to their helping spirits and to thank the spirits of the plants and animals they harvest. Shamans sing the songs of the ancestors. They sing away bad luck, pain, illness, and suffering. They sing to the waters of life, to a tree to honor its spirit, and to the invisible weavings of the web of life.

Sometimes songs are quite free flowing, and sometimes there are very specific songs to be sung in certain ways at particular times. For example, many shamans are experts in the use of the medicinal plants and plant spirits native to their area. When spirit prescribes an herbal treatment, it may direct the shaman to administer it in a very specific way through song.

Harnessing Energy

What you give energy to, you give life to. —Colleen Deatsman, *Inner Power*

What we give energy to, we give life to—no exceptions and no excuses. Shamans probably know this better than anyone. And if you are a shaman, you know that the fate of your people is the measure of what you're giving your energy to. With this type of serious responsibility guiding their way, you can bet that shamans pay attention to energy during every minute of every day and night. They know exactly where they spend their own personal energy, where their clients and the community spend it, and how to successfully garner it when needed.

In most shamanic cultures, only shamans are considered able to connect with, effect, and manage the flow of energies in both the ordinary and nonordinary worlds. Shamans source and harness energy with intention for all shamanic duties. This ability comes from strong relationships with helping spirits and the many lessons and experiences that are integral to the shamanic path. These essential experiences give the shaman the wisdom, perception, and impartiality to work effectively with all the diverse beings and energies in humanity, nature, and spirit. The shaman is, and always has been, master of energies that are beyond the understanding of most people.

Shamans cannot undertake personal healing, action in the world, and service to the community using only their personal life-force energy; they must harness the more powerful energies of nature, spirit, and the nonordinary worlds.

Energy is the fuel of life. Shamans know that, every day, people need to tap in to this source and keep it flowing. All people tap into this energy source automatically during deep, dreamless, delta sleep, and they get what energy they need to stay alive. Shamans need to be able access this source at will, both for themselves and for the people. Shamans cannot undertake personal healing, action in the world, and service to the community using only their personal life-force energy; it just is not strong enough. For shamans to effectively treat illness and cast out pain, suffering, and ill will, they must harness the more powerful energies of nature, spirit, and the nonordinary worlds. In order to create balance, harmony, and substantive change, shamans must learn how to interact with and harness the life-force energies of the web and beyond. Plugging into and channeling these energies for physical-world application are paramount for shamans.

In order to be effective, shamans must establish and maintain strong energetic connections and footholds with nature and the nonordinary worlds of spirit to fuel themselves. The work of shamans is to harness energy for their clients and the people, but in order to do so, shamans must be able to harness energy for themselves.

Shamanic work can be taxing and depleting. For one reason or another, it is not unusual for shamans to become drained or blocked energetically. When this happens, they need to take immediate steps to clear, reconnect, and refuel their energy. Energy blocks and drains are common among the people shamans serve, causing any number of disruptions in life, from illness and injury to exhaustion and discord. When shamans' energies are blocked or lost, it can be quite devastating to both them and the people, since the people rely on shamans to help them in their times of need.

Characteristic symptoms of energy loss or blockage are malaise, gross power/energy loss, low energy, loss of vitality, and feeling a spiritual void. Other symptoms include a deep dispiritedness and an inability to enter the nonordinary worlds of spirit or to connect with helping spirits or the spirits of nature. Failure to quickly correct these issues opens the door to opportunistic illness, mental problems, and addictions. Many shamans talk about these experiences as times when they lost their power or weren't able to doctor anymore. In these instances, the shamans must be able to tap back in to life-force energies and open the blocks so that the energy can begin to flow within and through them once again. They might consult another shaman for help, spend some time in solitude, or send themselves on a journey to a sacred site or on a vision quest to pray and petition for their power to return.

To prevent this kind of energy drain or disconnection, shamans have to diligently check in with themselves to see what they are giving life to. They must regularly, candidly explore their own energy expenditures and make the necessary adjustments to keep a healthy balance of output and input. Shamans pay attention to everything, throughout the day, catching small nuances and details in energy shifts within themselves and their environment. Many ask themselves questions such as: Where is my energy? How do I feel energetically? What am I doing, thinking, and feeling? How does my body feel? Is it sending me any messages through fatigue, pain, or discomfort? Am I experiencing any imbalances that I can affect right now? Where is my emotional, mental, physical, and spiritual energy going? What is it doing? Am I giving too much energy to others? Am I connected enough with nature, my helping spirits, and the energies of the nonordinary worlds of spirit?

Using Sacred Tools

> *[T]he round form of the drum represents the whole universe, and its steady strong beat is the pulse, the heart, throbbing at the center of the universe. It is the voice of Wakan-Tanka, and this sound stirs us and helps us to understand the mystery and power of all things.* —Black Elk, *The Sacred Pipe*

Sacred shamanic tools reflect, represent, augment, or derive from the shaman's power, spirit connections, and abilities to access these spiritual energies. Sacred shamanic tools are generally gifts from nature,

Figure 19

the spirits, or people in the community who recognize the healing and helping powers of the shaman. These gifts are not treated lightly. They are sacred objects that uphold and enhance shamans by keeping the energy channels open, the spirit connections strong, and the shamans cognizant of their power and responsibility to the people. Sacred shamanic tools focus and express energy received from nature, spirit, the web of life, and the shamans' helping spirits. They are used for divination, diagnosis, cleansing, entering into trance, ceremony, and healing. Depending on the culture and the individual shaman, drums, rattles, flutes, bells, bowls, feathers, mirrors, pipes, bones, runes, crystals, and various plant materials, like white sage or cedar (used for smudging), can be important tools in shamanic work.

Figures 19 to 24 show various shamanic tools used for specific purposes. The crafter and photographer of the Eagle Drum shown in Figure 19 shares, "This drum was made to honor Golden Eagle, who had healed my whole being." Figure 20 shows a shaman's mirror: a bronze *melong* that is integral to the ritual healing done by Tibetan shamans. It is used in divination, and the deities and spirits appear in the mirror to talk to the shaman. It also serves as a receptacle for the shaman's soul when he or she is on a shamanic journey. Figure 21 shows a gathering of several sacred feathers attached to bones to form a

Figure 20

brush, which is used to "brush away" illnesses and the negative influences that cause them as well as to smooth the luminescent energy body. Figures 22 and 23 show shaman's rattles, used to help the shaman shift consciousness, connect with spirits, and move energy. Figure 24 shows an eye curtain, used to help the shaman enter into and maintain the shamanic state within nonordinary reality. All of these tools are used, in varied forms and colors, in different cultures around the globe.

Figure 21

Representations of the shaman's power sources, helping spirits, and power animals can take many forms—amulets, fetishes, or carved statues; signs, symbols, or pictures; jewelry, gems, or stones; colors; numbers; mandalas; medicine bundles; prayer flags; beads; bells; herbs, seeds, leaves, or dried flowers; shells, eggs, bones, or feathers; objects from power places or objects gathered during important healing, training, or initiatory experiences. All such representations are considered sacred shamanic tools or power objects that shamans may keep with them and use in their shamanic practice.

Some sacred tools are inherited by the shaman, and some are given to the shaman by the community or shaman elders at various points in an initiate's training, initiation, or achievements. In some cultures, shaman elders hand down sacred tools during an initiate's training, at the end of training, or upon the impending death of the elder. Shamans sometimes create their own

Figure 22

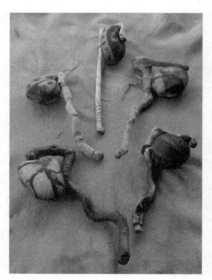

Figure 23

tools. In many cultures, shamans carve likenesses of their power animals or weave power into bark strips or grasses to create personal talismans that become working tools. Some sacred tools are made especially for the shaman by members of their community. For example, in some cultures, when shamans reach the end of their training and are ready to begin practicing their art, designated people in the community are commissioned to make the ceremonial clothing the shamans will need. In others cultures, a drum or rattle will be made for the new shaman. Some sacred tools are gifts from the spirits; for example, a shaman may use a bit of shattered wood from a lightning tree at a vision-quest site as a tool.

Sacred tools can also be things that represent a shaman at her very best or when he was pushed past his limits and was sustained or triumphed in some way. Looking at or holding the sacred object connects shamans with the powers that culminated in that influential event and reminds them that they are far more than meets the eye.

Some sacred tools are used for specific purposes. Others may be used for a variety of shamanic work, depending on the shaman, culture, and spirit guidance. For example, shamans may use a differ-

Figure 24

ent drum for a rite-of-passage ceremony than they would use for a healing ceremony, in order to draw in and weave specific powers and energies to produce a particular outcome.

All shamans know that their sacred tools are unique and special, and they get to know them on a personal level. Because everything—including a shamanic tool—is living and is a spirit, shamans talk to the spirits of their sacred tools and develop strong relationships with them, just as they do with their helping spirits, their family, and nature.

Spirit connections in the ordinary and nonordinary worlds also have a strong impact on the creators and crafters of scared tools. Navajo jewelry artist Jesse Monongye tells how, when he was a very young boy, he and his grandfather took a walk in the mountains and came across a bear. His

Because shamanic tools are living spirits, shamans talk to them and develop strong relationships with them.

grandfather spoke to the bear in Navajo, acknowledging the bear's strength and power and asking for its blessing and to pass safely. The bear retreated from its standing position and walked away into the forest. Today, this experience is part of Monongye's jewelry pieces—so much so that his pieces often depict images of bears. The bear is a symbol of the strength and power of his culture.[16]

Observation and the Art of Omenology

When we are not sure, we are alive. —Graham Greene

Shamans are students of life. Everything and everyone is a teacher, so shamans are always aware, awake, alert, and observant, both externally and internally, watching and listening without interpretation or judgment. Shamans see many things that others miss. By watching without opinion, shamans notice a natural flow, an inherent order, in how things work. Likewise, they notice when things are being manufactured, forced out of balance, or manipulated in some way. By watching everything and making observations, shamans learn about life, people, and energy.

Shamans notice the countless diverse ways in which nature and spirit are constantly communicating with them. Signs from nature, the things that people say, songs that pop into one's head or come on the radio, images in the clouds—all of these are messages bringing information to the shaman's conscious awareness.

Omenology is the name given to this practice of being aware. By paying attention to everything that happens around them, shamans become aware of internal and universal messages and signposts that mark their path through life. They know that these messages are available everywhere, within themselves and the world, so they use all their senses to notice and acknowledge the messages. Shamans not only notice the signs but also interpret them and integrate their messages using intuition and spirit guidance to call forth insights and knowledge that are helpful to the shamans or to the people.

Shamanism is, in its very nature, a practical way of living. Everything shamans do, they do for specific purposes. All of the practices described in this chapter—entering the nonordinary worlds of spirit by traversing a specific cosmology, honing of the senses, becoming a hollow bone, entering into trance, performing ceremonies, sharing stories of wisdom and healing, singing sacred songs, using sacred tools, and paying attention to life and omens—are methods that shamans use to garner energy and wisdom from all of the worlds in order to help themselves, the people, and the earth. Part four discusses how shamans use these practices for healing in the everyday world.

Part Four

Shamanism

and

Healing

Chapter 8

Shamanic Healing for Individuals

The more I am hollowed
by the fire, the more my ribs
spread like the tree of life.

The more I am washed
by the tears of others, the more
my heart rounds like an ocean shell.

The more stories I tell
of how one picks up another,
the more my hands open
like scoops for grain.

To be what others drink,
to be what others stand on
to reach what they love—
we should be so lucky
to be worn to this.

Mark Nepo, "What Sustains"

Healing and being of service to the people are the quintessential responsibilities of shamans. Shamans consider it an honor and a privilege, an extraordinary calling, to be of healing service.

That's not to say that healing service is always welcome or that it isn't difficult or overwhelming at times. But those times pass, and shamans know who they are because of the help they bring to the people. Deep, meaningful spirit guidance and direct revelation come to shamans because of the purpose and intention of their work. Spirits understand and take pity on humans and willingly share energy and power with shamans who endeavor to heal and help improve the lives of individuals, themselves, the community, and the world collective.

This chapter will introduce you to the shamanic view of and techniques for individual healing, and the next will explore how shamans are striving to heal the earth and humanity as a whole.

The Shamanic View of Personal Healing

Shamans work with helping spirits and energies to restore wholeness, balance, and power to persons, beings, and places. This restoration, in turn, heals physical difficulties.

Shamans see all physical, mental, and emotional illnesses as manifestations of spiritual and energetic imbalances; therefore, spiritual and energetic intervention can have an impact on any illness. Shamans whose responsibilities include healing, such as shamans called medicine men or medicine women, can conduct healing ceremonies for an individual, a family, a whole community, or the whole world. In these ceremonies, shamans enter into trance, journeying into the nonordinary realms, on behalf of their clients in order to meet with their own and the client's helping spirits. These spirits give them guidance about what spiritual, energetic issues underlie the client's illness and how the person's wholeness and power can be restored. The shaman's helping spirits usually give information about behavioral or lifestyle changes the client can make; spiritual,

> *The shaman works with helping spirits and energies to restore wholeness, balance, and power to persons, beings, and places. This restoration, in turn, heals physical difficulties.*

physical, and energetic practices the shaman or client can do; and wisdom for the shaman to share with the client to assist the restoration to healing and balanced living.

Shamans have a very different mind-set about healing than modern-day Western medical professionals do. Shamans see their clients as whole, animated beings, not broken, motionless pieces. They see a complete person—a physical body, a thinking mind, emotions, an energy body, and a spirit that moves within that person and all the others. Unlike most medical practitioners, shamans don't rely entirely on their training for their healing know-how. Instead, they enter the nonordinary worlds of spirit to connect with the powerful helping spirits for the guidance, energy, and power they use to diagnose the spiritual, energetic causes of each client's condition and to bring clients back into congruency and balance with themselves, their relationships, the environment, and the world. Their training is what enables them to make these spiritual journeys and obtain the knowledge and power they need.

Shamans see all physical, mental, and emotional illnesses as manifestations of spiritual and energetic imbalances; therefore, spiritual and energetic intervention can have an impact on any illness.

No matter what techniques they use, when shamans help a person heal, they deal directly with the omnipresent necessary energies for that purpose, and they understand that the effects soak into the client on all levels: physical, mental, emotional, energetic, and spiritual. Shamans first pull these energies out of nature and the nonordinary worlds of spirit. Then they channel the energies through themselves and transfer them into the client.

The healing experience is a cooperative and interactive process between the shaman, the client, any family or community members that may be present, nature, and all of the invoked and involved helping spirits. To overlook the participation of any of these integral parties is to miss the beauty and mystery of shamanic healing.

Shamans are known to help people heal and to make important life changes by working on a soul level. By spiritually treating painful experiences and the energetic imprints left by those experiences, a shaman can positively affect the person's spirit and energy field, resulting in regained equilibrium and health. Shamanic healing is practical, dynamic, and idiosyncratic. While the causes of each illness or imbalance are unique and nuanced, they generally fall into a few broad categories, each associated with traditional shamanic healing approaches.

To understand what really happens in shamanic healing, let's take a closer look at what soul/spirit energy is and why it is so valuable to the shaman and the people.

Spirit and the Energy Field

The physical aspect of the middle world is the place in the universe where energy moves the slowest and is at its most dense. When subtle, etheric energies coalesce, they densify and form the physical world and the beings within it. But they still consist of energy, and every physical being or object produces a characteristic energy signature—a soul or spirit, whose energy comes from the spiritual, unseen aspects of the other worlds. This soul, which radiates in and around the physical body, generates an energy field. Shamans who perceive this energy field describe it as a luminous, oblong sphere that permeates and surrounds the body, which is why it is sometimes called the luminescent energy egg.

Shamanic healing is a cooperative and interactive experience involving the shaman, the client, nature, and helping spirits. To overlook the participation of any of these integral parties is to miss the beauty and mystery of shamanic healing.

In humans, this energy field connects to the physical body via seven energy gateways, which many traditions refer to as chakras. The first four gateways are located vertically along the front and back of the torso, roughly six inches apart, and the upper three are aligned along the front and back of the throat, the forehead, and the crown of the head, respectively. These gateways sustain and regulate the energy field and its diverse vibrational energy layers.

Shamans believe that the health of a person's spirit and luminous energy field is just as critical to the health and well-being of that person as the health of the physical body—perhaps even more so.

If a person's soul is not whole or the energy field is dulled, blocked, destabilized, or punctured, the person will experience power loss, imbalance, and disharmony that will eventually cause malaise, illness, and disease.

Sluggish or Stagnant Energy Flow

Sluggish or stagnant energy flow in the luminous energy field is a common problem shamans see in their healing practices. It is one of the earliest warnings that illness may be on the way. Fortunately, it is usually an easy imbalance to fix.

Energy stagnation or sluggishness occurs when energy that should be flowing is impaired. Circumstances, such as stress, sometimes cause people to adopt behaviors that are unnatural or that cause an internal conflict, either of which can disrupt energy flow. Shamans help these people become aware of their behaviors, so they can make appropriate changes and reactivate the flow of the pooled energy.

Energy Blockages

Sometimes energy pooling over a prolonged period of time results in an energy blockage—energy that has congealed into an obstruction that keeps most or all other energy from flowing past or around it. Blockages are the energetic cause of many physical, mental, and emotional illnesses. They can be formed by all manner of things. Imprinting; conditioning; consciously and unconsciously stored emotions; physical, mental, and emotional trauma or abuse (real or perceived); toxic thinking; negative perspectives; unexpressed

Shamans believe that the health of a person's energy field is as critical to the health and well-being of that person as the health of the physical body—perhaps even more so.

and unresolved anger; unhealthy or self-destructive habits; addiction; and inflexibility are all examples of circumstances that can cause a long-term pooling of energy.

Shamans are able to identify energy blockages by scanning the person's energy field (through various techniques) and seeing, feeling, and sensing the blocked areas. Shamans also listen to the client describe his or her perceptions of the problems. Descriptions like, "I just can't get past it," "I'm stuck," or "I feel blocked" indicate that a blockage may be all or some of the problem.

There are three ways shamans treat this phenomenon.

Visualization

The first method is to energetically dissolve the blockage with the focused use of energy combined with intention and visualization. The shaman and the client work together to perform this visualization, talking out loud and sharing what they both see, sense, feel, and experience. Both close their eyes and focus on the locations of the blockage. They see the blockage in whatever form it presents itself and discuss its appearance. Then both shaman and client dialogue with the blockage, asking it how it came to be, any messages it has, and how to dissolve or remove it. Once they learn how to remove it, they use their intentions and all of their senses to visualize that action happening. For example, they might visualize little Pac-Man-like creatures eating up the blockage, the blockage opening like the gates of a dam, a snake consuming the obstruction, or an energy drill pulverizing it.

Circumstances, such as stress, sometimes cause people to adopt behaviors that are unnatural or that cause an internal conflict, either of which can disrupt energy flow.

The other two shamanic techniques used to resolve energy blockages are extraction, which is the equivalent of energy surgery, and dismemberment.

Extraction

Sometimes energies that become lodged in the human energy body appear to the shaman as energy forms that are somewhat more solid than a typical energy blockage. An unkind word, a specific or localized trauma, an injustice, things thrown at the recipient during a psychic attack, negative thought or emotion forms, uncrossed souls, heavy energetic imprints, conditionings, or old issues can all stick in the energy body. These energies can also reach into the physical field and cause localized pain or discomfort or sudden intense emotions that never seem to go away. These are called intrusions. (More about intrusions can be found later in this chapter.)

Shamans generally perform extractions while in a trance (or journeying) and with assistance from their helping spirits. This technique involves locating the intrusion and energetically removing it. Shamans scan their client's energy field and physical body, looking for any intrusions. When they find one, they speak with it and ask it to tell its story. Then they remove it any number of ways. For example, they might encapsulate the intrusion in energy; dissolve it; transmute it; or pull, scoop, suck, tease, or scrape it out of the energy field. Often, shamans will transmute or transform the energy of the intrusion by placing it in fire, a crystal, a bowl of water, or the earth. These natural forms dissipate the energy, taking it out of the client's world and transmuting it into energy that nature can recycle and use.

One way shamans address energy blockages is to dissolve them with the focused use of energy combined with intention and visualization.

Figure 25 shows a *phurba*, a sacred, hand-carved wooden dagger that shamans use as a tool for extraction. When used correctly, the

Figure 25

phurba takes out intrusions that cause illness and replaces them with the elixir of healing.

Once the intrusions are removed, the shamans fill the newly voided space with harmonious, healing energies from nature, their helping spirits from the nonordinary worlds, or the client's own pure, high-vibrational soul energy. Then they seal the energy boundary that surrounds and protects the energy field and the body.

Dismemberment

Dismemberment is a shamanic phenomenon that, on occasion, happens spontaneously to shamans, initiates, or journeyers. It is also a technique used as an initiation in many shamanic traditions and as a powerful healing method to address many issues. It can be used to remove energy blockages and intrusions, to cleanse energy, to remove illness, to cast away low vibrational or unhealthy energies, and to facilitate energetic organ transplants.

Dismemberment entails both the shaman and the client traveling to a power place in the nonordinary worlds and asking the helping spirits to facilitate a shamanic death for the client for the purpose of initiation or healing. During the journey, the shaman and the client will typically experience the client's body undergoing an extraordinary metaphorical death and dismemberment, while the person's actual physical body, in the ordinary world, experiences no pain or discomfort. Once bodyless, the client experiences what it is like to be pure spirit, energy, soul—free of the confines and limitations of the physical body and free to experience things on a soul level.

Before the shaman and client return to ordinary reality, the client's body is reassembled, or re-membered, minus any intrusions, blockages, or illnesses that were present before the journey.

In addition to clearing energy, this journey fosters a client's sense of connection to others, the web, the soul-self, nature, and the client's helping spirits in new ways. The dismemberment death is also known to release the stronghold of the ego and to allow the client to be reborn, reconnected to the web of life. The concept of a dismemberment journey may seem a little strange or frightening, but dismemberment is a safe, time-tested, and remarkably beneficial shamanic healing technique.

Energy-Boundary Leakages

Another energy problem that shamans see regularly is the loss of energy through a rip, hole, puncture, or split in the boundary of the energy field. When a person experiences trauma that might involve intrusions, possession, attachments, or soul loss, this energy boundary will appear to the shaman like swiss cheese, full of holes or gaps. When not fully intact, the energy boundary is not able to protect the person from energetic invasion or to contain the personal energy of the physical body and energy field.

When not fully intact, the energy field's boundary cannot protect a person from energetic invasion or contain the personal energy of the physical body and energy field.

To address energy leaks, shamans journey into nonordinary reality, connect with their helping spirits, and begin the process of searching the person's energy boundary to find where it is losing energy. When they find an energy-boundary leak, they ask it how it came to be, thus finding out if the cause is an ongoing problem. If the cause is a problem, habit, or circumstance that the client can address in ordinary, physical reality, shamans will tell their client so he or she can choose whether or not to allow that cause to continue reinjuring the energy field.

Once shamans understand the underlying cause or message of the leak, they and their helping spirits seal it up with energy. Some shamans see the leak sealing and healing like a skin cut healing, with the sides overlapping the injury and leaving the energy boundary leak- and scar-free. Some shamans knit the gaps together, while others weave energy in and around the open or weak areas. I see a rainbow vortex that swirls from the inside of the client out to the energy boundary, vibrating the entire layer, leakages and weaknesses included, into a healthy, vibrant shell.

Cords and Energy Links

Clients sometimes seek out shamans to help them disconnect energetically from another person when a relationship is unhealthy, unbalanced, or needs to end. When addressing these concerns, many shamans see energy links or cords connecting the client with the other person—cords that are draining energy from one or both individuals.

Generally, when shamans discover energy cords, they listen to the reasons for the existence of each one. Then they may energetically remove the cord, being sure to pull it from its connection point in each person, or cut the cord by envisioning a sacred shamanic cutting tool or knife cutting the cords away. They watch as the cords fall completely away, and then they fill the newly void space at each connection point with harmonious, healing energies from nature, the nonordinary worlds of spirit, and soul energy.

Intrusions and Foreign Energies and Entities

Intrusions are sometimes caused by inorganic entities or unhealthy thought or emotion forms. Those observing shamanic cultures often refer to these energies as evil spirits because the observers lack understanding of spiritual experiences and language.

Intrusions are sometimes caused by inorganic entities or unhealthy thought or emotion forms. To shamans, these energies are tenacious entities that like to partake of the energies and pleasures of a physical body but don't have one of their own.

To shamans, these energies are tenacious entities that like to partake of the energies and pleasures of living in a physical body but don't have one of their own. In cases where an individual is run down or traumatized, these entities can enter or attach themselves to the human energy body or dulled energy field. When this happens, the person may feel disconnected, not his or her usual self; experience a personality change; take on behaviors atypical to them; or become ill. Shamans watch for people in their community experiencing these kinds of symptoms. With clients, shamans listen to the person's descriptions of his or her experiences for signs indicating the client might be possessed, attached to, or under the influence of a foreign energy.

Depossession

If a foreign energy or entity is the source of a client's problems, shamans use a technique called depossession, extracting the energy or entity as they would an energy blockage. When they come in contact with the energy, they may experience a more intense exchange with it than they would with a blockage or intrusion. However, the end result is the same: the energy must leave. Energetic entities can be counseled, lured, charmed, driven off, commanded to leave, banished, or escorted to a new place.

Psychopomp

Spirits of the dead can also cause energy-field intrusions. Spirits of the dead can get stuck in the middle world for a variety of reasons. It may be that they aren't aware that their body is dead. Some are afraid of crossing from their earth life and the familiar lower, denser energy vibrations of the physical and nonordinary energies of the middle world to the higher, lighter energy vibrations of the nonordinary worlds (the lower and upper worlds). Because these nonordinary worlds are unseen, unknown, or taboo to many people in life, in death, their spirits often fear these worlds. Some souls that may want to cross over become confused about how to do so once they leave their physical bodies. Others have a story to tell, unfinished business to take care of, or a message to impart to the living. Some are unwilling to leave their loved ones. Some are unwilling to leave nature and the earth, or they choose to stay because they enjoyed living on earth, in the physical world, so much. In some cases, these spirits will attach themselves to the living.

Psychopomp is a shamanic technique for helping and encouraging spirits of the dead to cross over.

If shamans find that a spirit of a dead person is causing their client's intrusion, they encourage the spirit to cross over using a method called psychopomp. Usually, shamans just need to listen to the uncrossed spirit's story, encourage it to leave the middle world and cross over, and assist it by gathering the spirit's energy, removing it from the client's energy field, and giving it a gentle push toward home. (Home is either up into the light or down into the womb of the earth.) This relieves the client of the unwanted energies and frees the spirit to move on to the next world or its next physical manifestation.

Sometimes spirits of the dead do not want to leave or don't know how to go. In these cases, shamans call into the next world to bring the spirit's loved ones to this side of the light to help the uncrossed spirit move on. On rare occasions, the spirit is not able or is unwilling to cross over and can be escorted only as far as a holding place. Shamans see these holding places as healing places, where the spirit can rest, reconnect with helping spirits, and do the necessary releasing or healing work needed to move on later.

Power Loss and Dis-spiritedness

Sometimes helping spirits disengage from a person, or the person pushes them away consciously or unconsciously. Shamans refer to the resulting disconnection and spiritual power loss as becoming dis-spirited, or experiencing power loss. To help clients retrieve their lost power, shamans journey to the nonordinary worlds of spirit to find the disconnected helping spirits and reconnect them to the clients.

> *Sometimes helping spirits disengage from a person, or the person pushes them away consciously or unconsciously. Shamans refer to the resulting disconnection as becoming dis-spirited. The result of dis-spiritedness is spiritual power loss.*

Helping spirits may be lost for many reasons. When people do not recognize or honor their helping spirits' presence or guidance, the spirits may distance or completely disconnect themselves from those people. Disregarding one's destined path, misusing power, and persistently engaging in unhealthy behaviors can also cause spirit disconnection.

When people become dis-spirited, they experience a deprivation of power resulting in symptoms such as feeling lost, anxious, or disconnected from life. Other symptoms of power loss can include, but are not limited to, loss of purpose, choice, and direction in life; chronic fatigue; chronic illness; depression; anxiety or panic attacks; insecurity; inability to focus; vulnerability; weakness; ongoing misfortune; absent-mindedness; susceptibility to psychic attack; energy leakage; and other chronic problems. Power loss may also be the problem if people are having difficulty with their own personal journeys, meditations, or intuitive insights.

When a client presents these symptoms to a shaman, the shaman journeys on behalf of the client to meet with the shaman's and the client's helping spirits. In this journey meeting, the shaman seeks the exact diagnosis of the problem and the most effective course of action. If the power loss is a result of disconnection from spirit, the shaman seeks information about why the helping spirits left, petitions the helping spirits to return, reconnects the client with the helping spirits whenever possible, and re-creates the client's bridge to the nonordinary worlds of spirit. The client is then responsible for bonding with the helping spirits by honoring them in ordinary reality, visiting them during quiet meditation, and calling on them regularly for assistance with daily life.

Soul Loss

Since the soul transcends time and space, it carries the living-energy memories of all events and responses to those events, whether those events are celebratory, joyful, neutral, painful, or distressful. When humans have experiences that the soul or psyche views as traumatic, they can lose soul energy. This lost energy remains fixed in the event, but separate from the body, mind, and core soul. Pure, high-vibrational soul energy (sometimes in fairly large portions, called soul parts) drains away, fragments, is blocked from, is pushed away from, or splits off from a person's core soul, which resides in and around the physical body and energy field. The original traumas and the subsequent soul loss can be experienced consciously and unconsciously. Soul loss is a normal coping mechanism that helps a person's soul withstand a painful event. In psychological terms, this phenomenon is called dissociation.

A spiritual, energetic, emotional, physical, and psychological illness—soul loss is common and detrimental, causing power loss as well as mental and physical debilitation of all kinds and all levels of severity. Soul loss can be the primary cause of a current emotional, mental, physical, or spiritual issue or illness.

Sometimes people are aware that part of their soul has separated from their core soul. When recalling the causal trauma, they might describe watching it from above, as if they were floating on the ceiling above the action occurring below, or they might say they heard the sound of the event, such as a crash, yet didn't feel any part of what was happening to their bodies.

Soul loss can result from any type, level, or severity of perceived trauma, abuse, neglect, or abandonment such as: separation from one's family, community, or its protections, norms, and customs; an accident; an altercation with a predator or perceived predator; surgery; the breakup of a relationship; a dispute in a relationship (when one person holds on to a part of another person's soul and doesn't let go); extensive unhealthy substance use; witnessing a traumatic event; being involved in war; or experiencing the death of a loved one. Essentially anything that causes mental, emotional, physical, energetic, or spiritual energy loss and pain can trigger soul loss.

When humans have experiences that the soul or psyche views as traumatic, they can experience soul loss, in which pure, high-vibrational soul energy—called soul parts—separates from a person's core soul.

The trauma does not have to be considered severe to cause soul loss. It may also be induced through more subtle occurrences, such as when children are separated from their home and parents on the first day of day care; a respected teacher makes a hurtful remark; or people give too much of themselves and their energy to loved ones, their workplace, or their clients.

Soul loss leaves the person's body and energy field vulnerable. Its symptoms can include, but are not limited to, depression, anxiety, memory loss, addiction, mental and emotional numbness, an inability to fully participate in life, a weakened immune system, frequent or chronic illness, and feeling empty inside. If the lost soul energies aren't returned to the person, the empty void soon fills with less desirable energies that prevent the person from being healthy, whole, and fully functioning.

Retrieving lost soul energy and soul parts is the strong suit of many a shaman. As they do with other shamanic healing modalities, shamans enter into nonordinary reality using trance or journey techniques, connecting with their helping spirits, and—with this spiritual guidance—travel to the places in the ordinary world and nonordinary worlds of spirit where the soul energies and parts are waiting. They meet with, communicate with, and retrieve any lost soul energies or parts that are ready, willing, and able to return. Shamans may also meet soul energies that are not yet ready to return but that make their presence known for a later retrieval.

Lost soul energy and parts may be found anywhere, in any of the three worlds. Sometimes they are waiting in the places where they were left or lost; sometimes they are waiting in safe places, with helping spirits, in the spirit worlds. The client's soul self, the client's helping spirits, and the shaman's helping spirits guide the shaman to these places, or the helping spirits bring the lost energies to meet the shaman and client in a particular location that they are guided to travel to.

Soul energies and parts go to different places for many different reasons and vary significantly in appearance. It is important to understand, as the shaman does, that soul energies are pure, high-vibrational energy and left a person so they could stay that way. Many a shaman's story describes the tests the shaman was put through before these energies trusted the shaman enough to reveal their location, appearance, and story and allow the shaman to retrieve them.

Once shamans find the lost soul energy or part, they introduce themselves and their helping spirits, and allow as much time as the energy needs to become acquainted. The soul energies often have a message or a story to impart, and shamans listen to these in order to share them with their client.

The soul energies also include a gift that will return with them to the client. The gift is often a powerful energetic representation of a personal attribute, such as self-love, self-worth, personal safety, confidence, or the ability to trust and love another fully. That attribute was lost or compromised when the energy departed. The gift may be something the client remembers once having, but it can also be something new, something the client never knew he or she had but has now earned.

When the soul energy or part is ready to return, shamans reach out with the aid of their helping spirits and gather in the energies, sometimes holding the energies in their hands, sometimes carrying them in their heart, and sometimes placing them in a sacred vessel or crystal before transferring them to the client. Shamans usually blow the energies into their client's energy field through the client's solar plexus chakra, heart chakra, and crown chakra, or any other places the shamans are guided to blow into.

The shamans may then take a moment to watch the energies spread out, expand, and begin to reintegrate into the client. After a few more moments, they check with the helping spirits to see if there are any more energies or parts that can return in this journey. If there are, they repeat the process as many times as guided. If the helping spirits say that they are finished for the day, the shaman seals the client's energy field and fortifies the energy boundary (usually by shaking a rattle around the client), thanks all of the helping spirits, and returns to ordinary reality.

When the soul energy or part is ready to return, shamans reach out with the aid of their helping spirits, gather in the energies, and transfer them to the client.

Following the soul retrieval, there is a period of integration in which the returned energies settle back in to the core soul, the client becomes reacquainted with the returned soul energies, old wounds begin healing, and a new light appears inside of the client. This integration process often extends over several months.

Soul Wounding or Soul Entrapment

Shamanic soul retrieval can also be used for soul wounding. Also called soul entrapment, soul wounding happens when a person can bear a trauma but cannot process it. As a result, a bit of soul energy pools around the memory of the traumatic event, tying up a great deal of personal energy and soul attention—so much that sometimes the person's expression of soul and progression along his or her soul path is severely limited or eliminated all together. When shamans hear clients say such things as, "I just can't get over it," "I'm stuck with this," or "Every time I think of it, it all comes rushing back, and I'm there all over again," they know they may be dealing with a combination of soul loss and personal and emotional energy pooling.

Many of the symptoms of soul wounding are the soul pointing at the event, making sure that someone, either the conscious mind of the client or the shaman, is aware that there is energy lost or caught in that event.

Soul Hiding

Soul hiding is a shamanic technique that serves two unique purposes. One is to protect a person's soul energy or other vulnerable parts from damage or thievery, and the other is to help heal and strengthen vulnerable soul parts.

For many reasons, people place or find themselves in difficult and potentially dangerous situations. Military personnel, law-enforcement officers, refugees, war protestors, lobbyists, and people working slowly and carefully to get themselves out of an abusive relationship are all prime examples of people in such circumstances. For these people, soul hiding protects their soul energies from potential soul loss or damage from exposure to imminent dangers. With the assistance of the helping spirits, shamans can help these people temporarily release specified soul parts and hide them in a safe, sacred place until the danger has passed.

Soul hiding serves two unique purposes: protecting a person's soul energy or other vulnerable parts from damage or thievery, and helping heal and strengthen vulnerable soul parts.

Shamans can also help clients temporarily release vulnerable parts of themselves—physical, mental, emotional, spiritual—and take these parts to a sacred place for healing and strengthening. After a period of time specified by the helping spirits, the part is retrieved and returned to the client in a more powerful state. This technique has been used successfully to help people overcome depression, phobias, panic attacks, anxiety disorders, stress, addiction, and many illnesses.

Chapter 9

Shamanic Healing for the Collective Us

If you are coming to help us, you are wasting your time. But if you are coming because your liberation is bound up with ours, then let us work together.

Lilla Watson, Aboriginal elder, Australia

Shamans understand and operate from the precept of interconnectedness—the connection between everything that is so powerful that there is no separation, only oneness. Not only are people not separate from one another, nature, and the web of life, they are also not separate within themselves. Humans are spirits radiant with energy and purpose, a body designed to create and maintain perfect health, a mind that records data and events and helps people make choices, feelings that serve as guideposts, emotions that move people into action, and an energy field that receives needed energies while simultaneously keeping out dangerous ones. Many parts of the whole would not exist on their own. They work together in unison, harmony, and balance not only to form and sustain a healthy person but also to enable that person to affect his or her world.

Western technologies have nudged humans into compartmental-ized thinking and separation from their whole self. Modern medicine labels people as the ailment they have, not the person they are—they say, "the gallbladder in room #214" or "the DSM-IV code 296.44 Bipolar I Disorder, Most Recent Episode Manic, Severe with Psy-chotic Features." Physical medicine tends not to want to deal with mental or emotional issues, and psychology doesn't want to talk about physical ailments or spiritual revelations. In between is a whole lot of space that no one wants to address.

But it's not just the medical institutions that promote the idea of separation. In a world where people are busy rushing around from responsibility to obligation, from one activity to another, they have moved away from paying attention to their whole self and especially recognizing and honoring their spiritual needs.

Addressing and correcting issues of separation has become a rela-tively new area of work for many modern-day shamans.

Separation from nature is often the root cause of many spiritual and physical illnesses and emotional difficulties. It has become so pro-nounced that it even has a name, nature deficit disorder, and a book written about it, *Last Child in the Woods* by Richard Louv. Because stress and overwork are the ridiculous rulers of modern-day society and men-tality, people are finding it harder and harder to get outdoors and play. Humans have an innate need for a connection with nature, but that need is being circumvented by logical, left-brained, "produce and consume" mind-sets, beliefs, and behaviors as well as by walls and cubicles. The cumulative effect of this imbalance takes a serious toll, as people expend more and more energy without replacing it.

The solution from a shamanic perspective? Relax, let go, open up, play, and get outdoors.

Nature is full of genius, full of the divinity; so that not a snowflake escapes its fashioning hand . . . —William Beebe, *The Log of the Sun*

Wandering in nature feeds the soul and frees the mind for seeking. Seeking encourages wisdom. Wisdom is knowledge in action. When our wandering includes seeking, and our seeking includes wandering, vast worlds and limitless possibilities open to us. Wandering calms our mind. Seeking cultivates bare awareness. Bare awareness changes the complexion of our thoughts, feelings, beliefs, neighborhoods, parks, beaches, and forests, revealing internal and external treasures we've never before noticed. Our mind expands. Limits fall away. Our heart sings. The world becomes alive and animated. Nature speaks to us. We are one.

I am the river, I am the sea,
I am the forest, I am the tree,
I am the mountain, I am the stone,
I am the desert, I am the bone,

We dance in circles around and around
We dance in circles around and around

I am the elder, I am the new,
I am the nation, I am you,
I walk a fine line, I run with wolves,
I fly with eagles, I dance with fools,

I laugh in silence, I cry out loud,
I scream in anger, I stand too proud,
I am the mountain, I am the stone,
I am the desert, I am the bone,

We dance in circles around and around
We dance in circles around and around
We dance in circles around and around
We dance in circles around and around

—Barb Barton, "Circles"

As Barb Barton's shamanic song "Circles" so eloquently and beautifully depicts, we are not only who we think we are; we are also all things, and all things are us, combined, circling, and cycling through this experience called life. The universal law of correspondence speaks to this understanding: *as above, so below; as within, so without.* This law is not a belief unique to shamanism, but an ancient understanding that shamans have followed throughout history. And it is an understanding whose time has come.

In 2007, physicist Garrett Lisi presented evidence of this concept in his E8 "Theory of Everything."[17] Lisi is endeavoring to quantify something that shamans have known for thousands of years: separateness is an illusion, a deception of the times, our culture, and the conditioning of our life experiences and level of awareness. This illusion of separation makes people think that they are islands, unaffected by the world around them and not responsible for what they think and do. This treacherous illusion can adversely affect all those who share the planet and each other's lives, leaving people feeling abandoned, drained, and unfulfilled without knowing why. For many people, separation from one another causes energy and soul loss—common spiritual illnesses that modern-day shamans are called on to treat. Humans have an innate need to be part of a tribe, but they are being cut off from one another by four walls and locked doors. In his book *Friendship with God*, Neale Donald Walsch shares,

> *We are not only who we think we are; we are also all things, and all things are us, combined, circling, and cycling through this experience called life.*

> [E]very sadness of the human heart, every indignity of the human condition, every tragedy of the human experience can be attributed to one human decision—the decision to withdraw from each other. . . . I believe we know at the highest level that We Are All One. It is this supreme awareness that pulls us toward each other, and it is the ignoring of it that creates the deepest loneliness of the human heart, and every misery of the human condition.[18]

Many subcultures, tribes, and communities today and in the not-so-distant past operate as a whole entity focused on the continued existence and good of the people. Individual, team, and group accomplishments are celebrated, tragedies are shared, and families split workloads, raise children together, and cherish and learn from the elders of the community. In these communal societies, people know that they share energy and that the same energy that sprouts corn into plants to produce food also guides the caribou to migrate hundreds of miles and flows within and through everything and everyone. The people know that what happens to one person happens to us all, and that what we do to the earth and her beings, we do to ourselves.

Modern-day shamans around the globe are watching as people voluntarily and involuntarily destroy and resurrect this very fundamental precept of oneness. On one hand, people are choosing consciously or unconsciously to dissociate from nature, the helping spirits, each other, and themselves in the name of science and progress. Deforestation, drilling accidents, depression, anxiety, chronic illness, and dissatisfaction with life are a few of the visible manifestations of separation. On the other hand, a huge shift in energy and focus is bringing back our connection with nature, community, helping spirits, and self. Such things as grassroots organizations, gatherings to clean up the environment, peace coalitions, walking groups, running groups, bicycling groups, gardening groups, community-supported agriculture, book-study groups, and drumming circles are a few of the visible manifestations of this side of the pendulum swing. People involved in these activities report feeling healthy, having passion and excitement for what they are doing and for life, and feeling satisfaction in helping the world become a better place.

For many people, separation from one another causes energy and soul loss— common spiritual illnesses that modern-day shamans are called on to treat.

Modern-day shamans are often found in the midst of these groups, often leading them. Their helping spirits frequently guide them to recommend that clients suffering from separation issues engage in group activities, walks in nature, spiritual pursuits such as meditation or journeying, and play time.

If we want peace in our world, we've got to learn to care about one another. —Grandma Agnes Baker-Pilgrim

The Collective Dream

Somehow we always came back to the point that everything is a part of the whole. We are all connected, influencing the outcome of the future of our lives and the planet we are living on. What we think and how we act is not just a one time event and later gone. Every thought has a life by itself and every action has an effect that reaches far beyond what we can understand. —Grandfather Semu Huaute, Chumash medicine man

Shamans have long believed that the world is the way it is because humanity has dreamed it into being this way and holds it in place by continually dreaming the same dream through our thoughts, feelings, actions, words, agreements, and disagreements—consciously, unconsciously, or both.

In *The Four Agreements,* Don Miguel Ruiz, a Nagual from the Eagle Knight lineage in Mexico, explains:

> Dreaming is the main function of the mind, and the mind dreams twenty-four hours a day. It dreams when the brain is awake, and it also dreams when the brain is asleep. The difference is that when the brain is awake, there is a material frame that makes us perceive things in a linear way; when we go to sleep we do not have the frame, and the dream has the tendency to change constantly. Humans are dreaming all the time. Before we were born humans before us created a big outside dream that we call society's dream or *the dream of the planet.* The dream of the planet is the collective dream of billions of smaller, personal dreams, which together create a dream of a family, a dream of a community, a dream of a city, a dream of a country, and finally a dream of all of humanity. The dream of the planet includes all of society's rules, its beliefs, its laws, its religions, its different cultures and ways to be, its governments, schools, and social events and holidays.[19]

Shamans know that a new dream is possible and is, in fact, already in progress. Since everyone is collectively dreaming, each of us can, with awareness and proper action, change the dream if we choose. And we are, as the following four examples demonstrate.

The late Thomas Banyacya, pictured in Figure 26, was known to many as the Hopi Gandhi. He was a vigilant peace-keeper and called people to dream the new dream of what is called the Hopi Prophecy. In this translation of his teachings, which he presented during the Prayer Vigil for the Earth in Washington, D.C., between 1994 through 1998, he shares:

> Near Oraibi, Arizona, there is a petroglyph known as Prophecy Rock, which symbolizes many Hopi prophecies. . . . The large human figure on the left is the Great Spirit. The bow in his left hand represents his instructions to the Hopi to lay down

their weapons. The vertical line to the right of the Great Spirit is a time scale in thousands of years. The point at which the Great Spirit touches the line is the time of his return.

The "life path" established by the Great Spirit divides into the lower, narrow path of continuous Life in harmony with nature and the wide upper road of white man's scientific achievements. The bar between the paths, above the cross, is the

Figure 26

coming of white men; the Cross is that of Christianity. Here we see a line that represents a choice like a bridge joining the paths. If we return to spiritual harmony and live from our hearts, we can experience a paradise in this world. If we continue only on this upper path, we will come to destruction. The circle below the cross represents the continuous Path of Life.

The four small human figures on the upper road represent, on one level, the past three worlds and the present; on another level, the figures indicate that some of the Hopi will travel the white man's path, having been seduced by its glamour. The two circles on the lower Path of Life are the "great shaking of the earth" (World Wars One and Two). The swastika in the sun and the Celtic cross represent the two helpers of Pahana, the True White Brother. The short line that returns to the straight Path of Life is the last chance for people to turn back to nature before the upper road disintegrates and dissipates. The small circle above the Path of Life, after the last chance, is the Great Purification, after which corn will grow in abundance again when the Great Spirit returns. And the Path of Life continues forever.

The Hopi shield in the lower right corner symbolizes the Earth and the Four Corners area where the Hopi have been reserved. The arms of the cross also represent the four directions in which they migrated according to the instructions of the Great Spirit. The dots represent the four colors of Hopi corn, and the four racial colors of humanity.

And in a message to the United Nations in 1992, Banyacya said:

I have been interpreting for my people since 1948. At that time, in Shungopaavi village, Hopi leaders, Chiefs and Religious men met for two days and went into many of the Hopi prophecies and knowledge that has been kept within the religious societies ever since we came here many, many centuries ago. They selected four interpreters to carry their message of which I am the only one still living today. [Banyacya passed away in 1999, at age eighty-nine.] At the time, I was given a sacred prayer feather by the spiritual leaders. I made a commitment to carry the Hopi message of peace and deliver warnings from prophecies known since the time the previous world was destroyed by flood and our ancestors came to this land.

The main reason they are now bringing this knowledge out and sending us to different areas is to tell the people, to warn the people, to explain this to them, to compare our knowledge, to compare our languages, and to compare our religious tenets . . . so we will be able to find each other. That is to say, we, who are searching for the right way of living, the truthful and peaceful way of harmony with each other and with nature all around: the clouds, the rain, the animals and the plant life. We are all a part of it. We cannot break away from that. We are going to have to understand this so that we can look at each other. We are just like the trees out there . . . all different people with different languages, different colors and different ways of expression. We are just like any other part of nature that is around us. This we must understand. . . .

Nature, the First People and the spirit of our ancestors are giving you loud warnings. Today, you see increasing floods, more damaging hurricanes, hail storms, climate changes and earthquakes as our prophecies said would come. Even animals and birds are warning us with strange change in their behavior such as the beaching of whales. Why do animals act like they know about the earth's problems and most humans act like they know nothing?

In every continent are human beings who are like you but who have not separated themselves from the land and from nature. It is through their voice that Nature can speak to us. I have studied comparative religion and I think in your own nations and cultures you have knowledge of the consequences of living out of balance with nature and spirit. If we humans do not wake up to the warnings, the great purification will come to destroy this world just as the previous worlds were destroyed. It's up to all of us, as children of Mother Earth, to clean up this mess before it's too late.[20]

A similar call to dream the new dream comes from the other side of the earth, via messenger Angaangaq Angakkorsuaq, a shaman from Greenland. He is pictured in Figure 27, with the Qilaut, the Eskimo Wind Drum, during the 2009 Ice Wisdom Sacred Fire Ceremony in Greenland. He shares the following wisdom on his website:

> The greatest distance in the existence of Man is not from here to there nor from there to here. Nay, the greatest distance in the existence of Man is from his mind to his heart. Unless

Figure 27

he conquers that distance he can never learn to soar like an eagle and realize the immensity within. . . . Only by melting the ice in the heart of Man does Man have a chance to change and begin using his knowledge wisely.[21]

During the 1970s, successful economist and businessman (and now renowned author and shamanic teacher) John Perkins received yet another call for dreaming a new dream in South America. In his book *Shapeshifting: Techniques for Global and Personal Transformation*, Perkins shares the conversation that led him to participate in powerful shamanic teachings from the Shuar people—teachings that would ultimately change his worldview and his life.

It's foolish to believe this can go on forever. Our way of life is irrational and unsustainable. Young people like you are the hope. Yet you cannot learn from our universities—they're tied to the ideas of the past. You must look elsewhere. . . . Ever hear about men who change shape, use mystical techniques to turn themselves into trees or animals? The shapeshifters. . . . Techniques like that may offer the only hope for changing your—our—culture.[22]

This fourth example of dreaming the new dream comes from Dee Slate, a shamanic practitioner, teacher, and acupuncturist in Maryland. She is consciously creating a new dream as part of a class she is taking. She tells us:

As you may remember Merlin started in the future and lived his life into the past, bringing with him the wisdom and vision of the future. So, yesterday in class we were asked to begin our "Merlin." I had been racking my brain since the program started and couldn't think of anything big enough. So, yesterday, they told us to think of something we see that frustrates us or that we complain about, something that effects a lot of people. Then to write a news headline for June 27, 2020 of ourselves being honored in the White House (if it still exists) for creating something that addresses that problem. . . . So here is my headline . . . I was so excited and am still weeping with awe at the thought of this. I would love it if you all would envision this with me. (The honoring at the

White House part isn't that important to me, it was just part of the assignment.)

June 27, 2020, news headline: Deanna Slate was honored today at the White House for her project entitled: Council of Trees.

Council of Trees is a national organization which has its roots in indigenous wisdom. The council began with its members being trained by native elders from all over the country in the art of communicating with the trees (as well as other beings in nature). Today every single developer in the country must have approval from the Council of Trees before removing any trees for building, and in most cases alternative sites can be found where no destruction of natural resources is needed. In all cases where approval is granted the developer is also required to find another site to plant the exact or greater number of trees in a habitat that supports the same life they are removing for their building. The result of this project has guaranteed the continuance of the woods, forests and all their natural inhabitants for the future generations of Mother Earth.[23]

Just imagine what could happen when enough power dreamers wake up from their collective trance of indifference and choose to create a new dream of their choosing. And imagine what will happen when the surrounding energy forces, vibrating in tune to that call for help, add their power and energy.

There are miracles within our grasp. Do you dare change the dream?

All that we are is the result of what we have thought. The mind is everything. What we think, we become. —The Buddha

We don't know what the mysteries of life have in store for us. The key is to keep our focus on the spiritual work we each feel called to do, no matter what the outcome is. And to remember that it is our responsibility to dream through our words, thoughts, and daydreams the new fabric of reality as the old begins to unravel and dissolve. —Sandra Ingerman

Part Five

Personal Healing, Shamanism, and Being of Service: Your Calling

Chapter 10

Finding Balance in an Imbalanced World

Shamanism is far too important to be left in the hands of only the shamans.

Victor Sanchez, author and Toltec shamanism teacher

"The world is as you dream it," he (Numi, Shuar Shaman) said at last. He walked to the edge of the water. "Your people dreamed of huge factories, tall buildings, as many cars as there are raindrops in this river. Now you begin to see that your dream is a nightmare." He bent to pick up a stone. "The problem is your country is like this pebble." He threw it far out into the river. "Everything you do ripples across the Mother."

"How can I change . . . ? How can my people change this terrible situation we've created?"

His eyes held mine once again. "That's simple," he replied. "All you have to do is change the dream."

It sounded so easy.

"How long will that take?"

He glanced once more down the river. "It can be accomplished in a generation. You need only plant a different seed, teach your children to dream new dreams."

John Perkins, *The World Is As You Dream It*

We are in a time of great change and transition, and life can seem very precarious. Shamans understand that the world won't end; the earth is all powerful, and it will continue to live and re-green. It is the people who may be heading toward oblivion.

Indigenous prophecies from the Hopi, Maya, many lesser known tribes, as well as Nostradamus (who had esoteric/Druidic/Celtic shamanism roots) speak of this time as one in urgent need of change. The Anishinaabe people tell the prophecies of the Seventh Generation, a time for reclaiming all that has been lost. A change is coming. A change must happen. A change is happening whether people want to realize it or not. The shamans have known about this change for thousands of years. The shamans are being called to herald in this change, and they could use our help.

> *The loss of our connection to the earth and nature, to the helping spirits, and to one another, in addition to the violent ways we treat one another, the earth, and the animals, add up to insurmountable soul loss.*

The way we live, swinging on a limb so far out of balance and harmony, is taking a toll on not only our environment and the people, but also on our very souls. Personal, soul, and collective energy are being depleted on an individual and global basis every day. Yes, modern technology and modern living have made the lives of so many comfortable and safe. We no longer have to worry if we or our loved ones will freeze to death in the depths of winter, suffer from hypothermia during the monsoons, or run out of food from the nearby forests and streams. We don't have to worry about being the main course on the plate of a tiger or bear. But despite all that we have gained in comfort and safety, we are paying a dear price.

A world full of chemicals has created an epidemic of untreatable cancers and immune disorders. Farms, long depleted of nutrients, are producing food that does not feed our cells, leaving us nutritionally deficient; immune suppressed; susceptible to foreign invaders, such as allergens, bacteria, viruses, and parasites; and harboring a hungry feeling that leads to obesity and addiction. Religions devoid of spirit tell us how to behave, but they do not teach us how to live in connection and oneness with energy, the web, and divinity. The loss of our connection to the earth and nature, to the helping spirits, and to one another, in addition to the violent ways we treat one another, the earth, and the animals, add up to insurmountable soul loss. The symptoms of this emotional, energetic, and spiritual illness are visible everywhere: rampant depression, anxiety, feelings of worthlessness and emptiness, addiction, and the loss of passion for living are but a few. The shamans could use our help. The people could use our help. We could use our help.

As children, we all came into this world with a special gift—a natural soul fullness, a magical creative spirit that saw and believed in helping spirits and the nonordinary worlds of spirit. Do you remember? Before you were encouraged to replace your naturalness with logic so you could fit into a rational, egocentric, industrial, fashionable world, your spirit experiences were as real and potent as anything in the ordinary physical world. The childlike innocence and receptiveness that allowed you to be approachable and sensitive to spirit connections and interactions back then are no different now. They are still there, simply underground.

This soulful exuberance is depicted in Figure 28, an illustration from the children's book *The Legend of Michigan*. Here we see the Little Warrior

The way we live, swinging on a limb so far out of balance and harmony, is taking a toll on not only our environment and the people, but also on our very souls.

dancing in the sky fire that the North Wind created in a failed attempt to frighten him away, while Gitche Manitou, the Great Spirit, looks on. This young warrior knows these spirits are real and that he can eventually make friends with the North Wind.

Figure 28

Every living being has a beautiful energy field and a natural, already intact connection with all of the energies around them (the web of life). You probably knew this as a child, but began to forget your connections and your innate skills for staying connected with energy and spirit as you got caught up in daily life. The pressures of early imprintings, societal conditioning, fitting in with friends, academic learning, the quest for achievement, making a living, excelling in our careers, raising children, and so on capture our attention and direct our behaviors toward satisfying the external aspects of making our lives happen. Balancing the Quicken spreadsheet and increasing our productivity begin to take priority over talks with friends, deep-breathing meditations by candlelight, walks in the woods, or gazing at a grasshopper with our wide-eyed child, or child self. Understandably, we have huge responsibilities. But little do we know that the spark of magic from our childhood, which kept us connected with the unknown then, still keeps us connected with life-force energies that we could hugely benefit from if we were to consciously and graciously access them now.

Shamanism offers us reconnection. It is a simple path that involves cultivating wholeness, balance, and the sacred in both spiritual practice and in everyday life.

Unfortunately, most of us, bombarded with constant stress, busyness, and a lack of awareness and know-how, over time develop patterns and behaviors that dangerously drain away soul and personal energies. We may think we are safe and secure in the illusions of our society's technology, behind the vinyl siding of our comfortable homes, but we are turning away from the natural sources of life and casting away the powerful primal energies that are available to help us. The time has come to save ourselves.

The solution is really quite simple: we need to reconnect.

Shamanism offers us an opportunity for reconnection. It is a simple path that involves being aware of, unveiling, and cultivating wholeness, balance, and the sacred in both spiritual practice and in everyday life. It takes no extra time out of your day to notice the messages of spirit and your soul and to observe what is really happening within and around you. Shamanism is merely a different mind-set. You do not need to move into the wilderness or to a certain location, or wear a wolf skin or a bracelet of bones to utilize the practices of shamanism. You do not have to practice someone else's ceremonies and rituals or pray at another's sacred sites. (In fact, doing so is adamantly discouraged unless a reputable person teaches you and gives you permission to perform the practices or to visit the sacred places of his or her culture.)

To practice shamanism in modern culture and our own home environment, we need only wake up to our awareness of self, nature, life-force energy, and spirit and reap the rich experiences available to us in each moment.

Though shamanic practitioners may choose to learn from teachers of different cultures, locations, and belief systems, they must ultimately integrate their learning into their own personal practice and lives in their own culture and environment. "Modern shamanism is not a practice of taking or borrowing someone else's religion or spiritual beliefs, nor does it involve copying the ways of the Mexican Nagual, the Lakota Medicine Woman, African Dagara Healer, or Peruvian Shaman," I wrote in my book *Seeing in the Dark*. "There is no need to imitate. The practice of shamanism is intimately personal and unique to every individual practitioner. Animism, the Web of Life, Spirit, and sacredness are omnipresent; they are everywhere, in everything, and belong to everyone."[23]

Shamanism is universal. The practices and principles can and are being applied around the world in many diverse cultures. To effectively practice shamanism in modern culture and our own home environment, we need only wake up to our awareness of self, nature, life-force energy, and spirit and reap the rich experiences available to us in each moment. By opening ourselves to learning from the all and everything in our lives, we can heal ourselves, retrieve our lost soul energy, and be of service by being a balancing and healing force in our relationships and the world.

We have seen the ripple effect of greed and power that is out of balance. Imagine the ripple effect of balance and healing.

———————————————————————

She knew . . .
before everyone else
she knew

As a child she heard
and felt things
In people
their homes
in places
she knew.

The Unexplainable and
just plain weird
the good and the bad
she took it on
she took it in
she looked at it
sometimes digested it
she knew

She didn't fit
She threw fits.
She felt weird.
Because

No one could explain
this part of life to her.
How do you explain
the unexplainable?
She hid it well
kept this secret
for a very long time.

Years later, now a young woman
Dad left her house
She felt it in her bones
the pain of never seeing
her Daddy again.
She cried all day.
Weeks later
the boating accident
then the stroke.
He's never been the same since.
She knew

Sitting in the meeting
the urge to leave.
Her child was in trouble
could she be imagining things?
She rushed home to find
Little girl and sitter
locked out of the house
in a thunderstorm
for over an hour.
She unlocked the door
daughter scared for her life
leaped into her arms.
She knew.

Dreaming
she saw her sister
sick and ill.
she woke up crying
two months later
the truth is revealed
about the tumor.
She knew

Finally one day
she visits The Healer
filled with spirit, laughter and joy.
Who became the mentor, teacher and friend
Re-birthed her gift of knowing
breathing in the truth "I believe in me" and
"I forgive myself for not believing-
I know what I know."

And so began the journey
to be okay,
with the knowing.
That comes and goes
Flows like the Tides
She knows . . .

—Michele Bailey-Lessirard

Chapter 11

Your Personal Shamanic Practice

A musician must make music, an artist must paint, a poet must write, if he is to be ultimately at peace with himself. What a man can be, he must be.

Abraham Maslow

Your Calling

Perhaps at this point you are recognizing or questioning your own call to shamanism. What is it that interests you or draws you to shamanism?

The same types of callings that bring traditional shamans into practice—a life crisis, being chosen by shaman elders, or an undeniable internal draw—could be calling you into practice, too. Sometimes these callings come as one big event, or successive events, or a combination of the two.

Are you currently, or have you ever, experienced a life-crisis calling? An illness, injury, accident, mental or emotional upheaval, personal near-death experience, or the near death of loved one can be a powerful motivator prompting you to seek out healing and spiritual guidance from shamanic practitioners or by direct revelation from your own helping spirits. It is often said in many traditions, "Healer, heal thyself." When you do and then become of service to others, you are known as a wounded healer. It has been well documented that wounded healers maintain their best personal health when they are being of service to the people.

Self-healing is easier said than done, and yet it is within each person's power. Sometimes it is the very thing that wakes you up to yourself and your own powers. The call to heal yourself is an individual, private cry for help that is sometimes so devastating that others who have not had this experience are unable to understand it. Many who have experienced this call do not even understand it themselves. It is a frantic call for delivery from pain and suffering—a call so desperate you are willing to give up almost everything for it, including clinging beliefs, destructive thoughts, and toxic behaviors. It is the very thing you need to reconnect with your inner self, personal power, luminescent energy field, thoughts, choices, feelings, emotions, physical body, and spiritual needs.

> *Self-healing is easier said than done, and yet it is within each person's power. Sometimes it is the very thing that wakes you up to yourself and your own powers.*

Sometimes a life crisis appears as a cosmic two-by-four, a spiritual, invisible "board" that your soul and spirits whack you over the head with when you aren't getting an important message or have fallen away from your soul's path. Cosmic two-by-fours appear as difficult life situations, unresolved emotions and feelings, or as physical fatigue or pain.

Have you ever been told by someone, perhaps a psychic, astrologer, healer, or respected spiritual friend or teacher, that you have special gifts? Being chosen by elders is another way shamans and practitioners are called by spirit. Parents, family members, family friends, teachers of all kinds, spiritual mentors, and spiritual teachers can help you see the internal light and soul illumination that lives within you and indicates that you have been touched by spirit. Elders can also confirm the call from spirit that you may be confused about or reluctant to answer.

Do you experience mysterious phenomena that seem to connect you with Spirit and the shamanic way of living? The call of spirit

may come in subtle ways that seem outside of you but are actually coming from your soul, like a book about shamanism falling off a shelf, a strange draw to websites about shamanism while you are surfing the Internet, or the topic of shamanism coming up during your visit to the psychic reader. Sometimes your call is a big event in which your spirit takes over and lets you know it exists, has power, and wants you to let it shine. It can be an extraordinary, profound, magical experience that makes you aware there is more to the universe than you can see, or it can be a powerful experience of living through something that likely otherwise would have killed you or drastically changed your life. Many people who have had these experiences speak of themselves *Parents, family members, friends, teachers, healers, and spiritual mentors can help you see the soul illumination that lives within you and indicates that you have been touched by spirit. Elders can also confirm a call from spirit that you may be confused about or reluctant to answer.*
as recipients of divine intervention, and the experience makes them want to know more about life beyond the ordinary physical world and how and why spirits interact with humans.

Do you experience an undeniable internal draw toward shamanism? This calling can be subtle or profound. It may begin as quietly as an intellectual interest in shamanism. Many an anthropologist has become a shamanic practitioner this way. It may begin as the desire to find a spiritual practice and way of living that has meaning, depth, and substance. Sometimes the calling seems to come from deep within and first appears as a subtle inner voice whispering intuitive insights by way of inner knowings and gut feelings. And sometimes, you find yourself overtaken by dreams, visions, experiences, signs, messages, and omens that propel you toward the shamanic way of living.

For many, the call to shamanism, the shamanic path, and the evolution that takes place within them throughout a lifetime of shamanic practice is a homecoming. In modern times, this call and the need to practice shamanism can seem as strange as being abducted by aliens, yet so familiar, it feels as if you have embarked on this path a million times.

Many theories attempt to explain the undeniable calling and coming-home feeling that so many people around the world are experiencing right now. Some think; feel; have been told by a psychic reader, teacher, or healer; or have been shown by their helping spirits that they have been a shaman, spiritual leader, or healing practitioner in another lifetime. Could be. Some think that another part of their soul is fulfilling similar roles in a parallel universe. Could be. Some think the time has come for people to wake up, become more aware and conscious, so that together we can make important shifts for humanity, the earth, and her inhabitants, and that is the reason they are being called into shamanic practice. Could be. Some just know, this is it, and the time is now. Some aren't so sure. The inner draw plays tag with their ego, and the two dance around each other, trying to decide who is in charge and where they go from here.

Learning by Doing

When we understand that the best and quickest way to achieve all of our goals and to live the life of which we have dreamed is to assist others in achieving their goals and living the life they have dreamed, we will have found the key to lasting happiness. —Neale Donald Walsch, *Happier Than God*

For many, the calling to shamanism begins with personal healing or the desire for a deep, meaningful spiritual practice. Your quest may propel you on a journey of self- and spiritual discovery that usually begins with developing observation skills, exploring nature, and connecting with the nonordinary worlds of spirit.

Sometimes dreams, visions, experiences, signs, messages, and omens propel you toward the shamanic way of living.

Every person has the ability to observe with bare awareness and connect with nature, the web of life, and spirit. Because of certain life experiences and learning, you may have lost or stifled your natural ability to connect. Adults often frown upon our natural affinity for daydreaming or talking about invisible friends, so we learn to avoid discussing or to block these abilities. But you already have the innate, natural ability to connect; it is easy to reopen the doorways and become receptive once again. You need only cultivate, activate, and enhance these natural skills.

As described in chapter 7, in this state of mindful, bare awareness, shamans access their felt sense, a potent faculty for perceiving energy and spirit. The felt sense is the amalgamation of all of the feelings, sensations, and realizations that shamans experience at any given time. You have a felt sense, too. With practice, you can become conscious and aware of what you are feeling everywhere in your physical body, everything that you are thinking and feeling, what is happening with you energetically, what you are sensing intuitively, what is happening around you, and how spirit is interacting with all of these things at once. By using your felt sense to take in the whole, unedited picture at all times, you can see the bigger picture. This may seem a bit overwhelming or complicated. But I assure you, it is a very natural occurrence, and once you begin to practice using your felt sense, your innate abilities will kick in.

Every person has the ability to observe with bare awareness and to connect with nature, the web of life, and spirit. You need only cultivate, activate, and enhance these natural skills.

To become your own shaman and a shaman in service of others involves relaxing into these natural perception abilities and allowing yourself to become an instrument of communication between the nonordinary worlds of spirit and the ordinary world. In order to be a clear channel for this communication, you must do the internal work of clearing away things that limit you, such as personal attachments, detrimental behaviors, unhealthy mind-sets, and energetic blockages and intrusions. This clearing not only brings your body back into balance, facilitating healing on all levels, but it also allows you to become a hollow bone, facilitating spirit expression.

The world is a manifestation of the web and is in itself an intelligent being that communicates with us in every moment. By observing and listening to these subtle messages, you will gain key information and insights into yourself and the world. By paying close attention to life and the signs, messages, and omens that come into your world through a myriad of ways, you can continually check yourself to see how clear the channel is.

Shamanic practitioner Gretchen Crilly McKay, pictured in Figure 29, underwent extensive tests of these skills before she was initiated as a sangoma during her training in Africa.

"My tests and the rituals of initiation were all on Saturday, with the attending sangoma dancing throughout the day and also walking with me from the place I was being secluded in between tests," she says. "In the photo, we are all celebrating because I had successfully completed all the tests set before me (finding my hidden goat, finding the hidden goat's bladder and skin, and being cut and infused with sacred *muthi* [herbs] after a water ceremony). We danced like this Saturday afternoon and most of the day on Sunday. It was a magical celebration of the sangoma tradition, and the others were rejoicing with me at the successful completion of my training."

Figure 29

> *To become your own shaman is to allow yourself to become an instrument of communication between the nonordinary worlds of spirit and the ordinary world.*

Reconnecting with the powerful healing energies and messages of nature is a part of personal healing and living a shamanic life. Your inner nature is not separate from the outer nature of your world. You may not think you are a nature person, but that does not make you any less a part of nature. Wild nature is the pure expression of undiluted life-force energy and the web of life in the physical world. By deeply observing nature, we can learn about efficient energy use, and through training, we can learn how to draw this energy in to use in our own healing process.

Learning how to enter into trance or the dreamtime to take a shamanic journey will most likely be an important part of your shamanic training. Journeying is a helpful tool for healing, harnessing energy, receiving spirit guidance, clearing away blockages and limiting or self-defeating behaviors, and bringing your self into balance and wholeness. By using tools and techniques such as drumming, rattling, rhythmic percussion, music, dancing, chanting, singing, specific breathing tech-

The Hollow Bone

nologies, or entheogens, you can learn to enter into nonordinary reality to access spiritual guidance and healing.

There are many ways you can learn to journey. Traditional and nontraditional, indigenous and nonindigenous teachers and practitioners offer seminars, classes, workshops, retreats, and apprenticeships. Some practitioners or guides, often referred to as sponsors, lead trips to areas where indigenous shamans are sharing their knowledge. Books, compact discs, and distance, online, and correspondence classes are other common ways to learn journeying. (Resources to explore are listed in the back of this book.)

Your inner nature is not separate from the outer nature of your world. You may not think you are a nature person, but that does not make you any less a part of nature.

How you learn to journey is a personal and individual choice. Some people prefer to learn individually at home or in nature in connection with their helping spirits, with or without the guidance of a learning tool such as a book or compact disc. Some people prefer to learn with a teacher or mentor in a group setting. Some people believe you should not learn how to journey on your own. Some people believe the only way to learn is on your own, directly following guidance from the spirits. Once again, there are no rules in shamanism, and what works for you may or may not work for another.

Once you have learned how to journey, there are infinite ways to use it. Simply by stating your intention, you can go anywhere and do anything with the guidance and assistance of your helping spirits. Even the sky is not the limit in journeying. Anything, including traveling beyond space and time, is possible, so be creative and follow your needs, intuition, and spirit guidance.

When you return from a journey, you may feel joyful and light. This feeling is known as shamanic ecstasy, a term used to describe the high-vibration energy boost and euphoric physical high that many journeyers experience after being in trance. The high felt by journeyers is often described as exquisite, peaceful yet energizing, and otherworldly. Journeys are magical travels into the mysterious, where the journeyer connects with energy that vibrates at a higher frequency than that of the ordinary world. The feelings brought forth by the energy connections are intense, pleasurable sensations that journeyers can tangibly feel throughout their entire body. Upon returning from a journey, the journeyer is both tranquil and supercharged at the same time.

Just as the type of calling varies from practitioner to practitioner, so do ways practitioners apply what they learn. One person's illness (a life-crisis calling) may be a call to do his or her own personal healing in connection with the helping spirits. Another may respond to the same call by participating in healing sessions with a shaman/shamanic practitioner and then train to become a shamanic practitioner.

One individual may respond to their undeniable internal draw by becoming a shamanic practitioner and working with others in a healing capacity. Another may begin lobbying for the protection of the environment based on an elder's call to connect with spirit.

If people are willing to contribute to the greater good, get in the trenches, and make a difference using spirit guidance, then they are shamans. Shamans believe that to heal oneself and to live in balance and harmony is a great gladness, and being afforded the opportunity to be of service and to help others and the world is a great honor.

Putting Information to Use

Enlightenment, or illumination, is not the intention of studying or practicing shamanism, living a shamanic life, or being a shamanic practitioner, but it is often what happens as you embrace and live a life of soul and spirit connection.

Once you have learned how to journey, there are infinite ways to use it. Anything, including traveling beyond space and time, is possible.

To be your own shaman and a shaman in service of others, you must bring the wisdom conveyed by the signs and omens of the ordinary world and the lessons you learn from your nonordinary-world journeys into your real, everyday life through practical understanding and action. Putting this information to use is crucial to your personal practice, health, and life.

How successful your journeys are and how well you read the messages of the ordinary world are subjective evaluations. It is important not to judge your experiences, but to sit with what happened or is happening for you. Use your felt sense to notice how an experience feels on all levels. Notice what images or sensations stand out, and then notice what is underneath those. Ask yourself what messages or meanings ring true, and then sit quietly and sense the answer with your whole being. This process will not only help you understand what just occurred or is occurring, but will also help you hone your senses and see in the dark.

Spirit messages and your journey's meanings may be very clear, simple, and easy to understand, or they may be puzzling. It is not unusual for spirit to communicate with humans using metaphor or experiential imagery, which many find difficult to understand. These images and metaphors are a unique language between you and your helping spirits that develops and becomes clearer over time. Some say this way of communicating is based in the language of the spirits and that it is our job to learn how communication with the spirits takes place. Spirits generally do not teach or share information in the clear, direct format many school-educated Westerners are used to receiving information in. We must learn to stretch our minds, expand our possibilities, and use our gut feelings, wits, senses, and intuition. Some say this way of communicating is based in our personal dream language; they say we already know how to communicate this way, and we just need to use all of our faculties, not just our logical mind, to understand what's being said.

To be a shaman, you must bring the wisdom conveyed by the signs and omens of the ordinary world and the lessons you learn from nonordinary-world journeys into your real, everyday life through practical understanding and action.

If the messages or teachings you receive are unclear to you, sit with the information and the details of the experience and let them simmer within you. Messages and journeys can be interpreted in countless different ways, so use your felt sense to see if you feel an internal resonance with your analysis. You may also choose to journey to your helping spirits and ask for clarification. Don't hesitate to go to the source for more in-depth understanding. You do have to do your own work, but you are not doing it alone.

You may also ask for dreams that will clarify the experience or information you receive. Dreams and journeys are very similar—sometimes one and the same—augmenting and leap-frogging one another. Asking your helping spirits to provide you with more signs, omens, and messages to clarify your understanding is also an option.

In a world wrought with competition and one-upmanship, it is important not to compare your experiences with those described by others in books, groups, or workshops. Since all personal practitioners are individuals, with different levels of development and different life experiences, no two journey interpretations will be alike, even two interpretations of similar journeys. Individual journeyers must interpret their own journeys based on the relevance to their intention, life experiences, and spiritual experience.

Spirits generally do not teach or share information in a clear, direct format. To communicate with them, we must stretch our minds, expand our possibilities, and use our gut feelings, wits, senses, and intuition.

Bouncing journeys and interpretation ideas off of others is a good idea as long as you remain true to your inner knowings about the journey. Others may have intuitive hits that can help you with your interpretation, or they may be wholly incorrect. If you choose to share and ask for interpretation help, consider the ideas you receive, but then form your own conclusions.

It is also important not to judge your spiritual messages and journeys, but to sit with them and see what comes into your awareness. Your experiences are for you and are perfect for you, whatever they may be.

You are in charge of your life. It is up to you to interpret spirit information and to use it in your life as you deem appropriate. I recommend that you do not make any major life changes based on journey information without first checking if it matches your own internal resonance. Also ask to receive substantial ordinary-world confirmation, and take plenty of time to gather more journey information and to judiciously consider the guidance before making the change. Spirit is the guidepost, the illusion breaker, and the truth revealer. You are the decision maker, and when you are being truly open and honest with yourself, you know best how to utilize spirit and journey information. Though you may harness energy and glean guidance from the web and helping spirits, you are the one who holds the power to do something significant with that energy and guidance. If you are in service to others, it is important that you also share this mind-set with your clients. They are in charge of their life, and all decisions are theirs to make.

It is important not to judge your spiritual messages and journeys, but to sit with them and see what comes into your awareness. Your experiences are for you and are perfect for you, whatever they may be.

A helpful awareness tool is your truth spot, the specific way you sense truth and untruth in your body and felt sense. Once you find your truth spot and hone your ability to use it, you will be able to discern your truth even when your mind is unsure or your emotions are clouding your judgment.

To find your truth spot, first sit quietly and clear your mind. Feel yourself relax. Inhale deeply and slowly, allowing your emotions to calm with your exhalation. As you sit quietly, bring feelings of peace and calm to your center through your breath and intention.

Now make a statement to yourself that you know to be true, and notice how you feel in response to hearing that truth. Note all of the sensations that you have in your body and the exact spot(s) within you that resonate with the truth of this statement.

Then make an untrue statement. Note the difference in the sensations within you and note the exact spot(s) in your body where the untruth registers. Each person is individual; therefore, your spots and sensations will be unique to you. Practice using these spots to heighten your awareness of truth and untruth until you are comfortable trusting your internal discernment skills. Note the differences in your accuracy and inaccuracy at different times and when you are addressing different shadings of the truth. Very quickly, you will find that you are able to access this ability in the course of your everyday busy life. Truth will always hit your truth spot, just as untruths will always hit your "untruth spot." In this

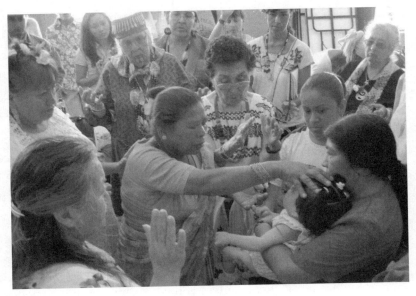

Figure 30

same way, you can also unerringly determine right from wrong and healthy from unhealthy.[29]

Sharing the idea of truth and untruth spots with your clients will help them connect with their own sensations and discern appropriate action for themselves, which is a valuable part of owning their power and being responsible for their life and healing.

Putting Energy to Use

Shamans are energy workers. They work with their own energy fields and those of their clients, and they work to conserve and harness energies. Aama Bombo (whose name means "Mother Shaman") is a renowned shaman in the Tamang tradition in Nepal. She embodies the goddess Kali and treats as many as one hundred patients a day, often conducting dramatic healing rituals long into the night. Aama is a member of the International Council of Thirteen Indigenous Grandmothers. Figure 30 shows her doing shamanic energy healing to help a child during a gathering of the Grandmothers in Oaxaca, Mexico, in 2006.

Those who can see the human energy field may also see the seven major chakras; seven or more auric layers, energy layers that extend out from the physical body and that match the chakras in vibration and color; and the energy boundary, which efficiently monitors energy input and output when it is healthy and intact. Some also see energy grids and meridians within and around the physical body and energy field.

Many shamans believe that the energy field is an emanation of our spirit that naturally connects with other spirits and energies, drawing in the life-force energy we need to sustain and revitalize us. For most people, the energy field attracts this life-force energy automatically, without their conscious awareness. For shamans, intentionally drawing in and utilizing life-force energy is a part of their daily practice. Many of the healing practices presented in chapter 7 involve cleansing the energy field or refilling it with power.

There are a couple ways that you can cleanse and power-fill without special training. By journeying into the nonordinary worlds, meeting your helping spirits, and asking for their help, you and they can immediately bring about the change and healing you need. The spirits are known to vibrate at a higher frequency than humans, especially ill or depleted humans, and they will increase your vibration just by being present with you. The energies of the nonordinary worlds are also of a much higher vibrational rate than human energy, and entering those worlds can bring about the change you need.

By journeying into the nonordinary worlds, meeting your helping spirits, and asking for their help, you and they can immediately bring about the change and healing you need.

Entering a sacred healing medicine place in either the physical world or the nonordinary worlds is another powerful way you can change your vibratory rate to facilitate healing and bring about balance and wholeness. A sacred healing medicine place is anywhere, real or imagined, that you feel whole or where your soul sings. In the physical world, these places are called power places. They are sometimes well known, but often those who live near them keep their locations secret. When you're looking for them, the locals might tell or show you where to find these spots if you ask with the right intention and a humble heart. The same is true in the nonordinary worlds, where your helping spirits are the locals.

If you can't go to one of these spots in the physical world, you can make a shamanic journey there.

A sacred healing medicine place is anywhere, real or imagined, that you feel whole or where your soul sings.

Sitting in the vortex of energy found in a sacred healing medicine place will allow high-vibrational energies to infuse your body and spirit. When you reach your desired sacred medicine healing place, take in a deep breath, let it out, let go, relax, and bask in the powerful energy. The experience is like soaking in a hot mineral bath of pure life force.

Chapter 12

Connecting with Other Shamans

Maybe, it's more like you said before, all of us being cracked open. Like, each of us starts out as a watertight vessel. And these things happen—these people leave us, or don't love us, or don't get us, or we don't get them, and we lose and fail and hurt one another. And the vessel starts to crack open in places. And I mean, yeah, once the vessel cracks open, the end becomes inevitable. . . . But there is all this time between when the cracks start to open up and when we finally fall apart. And it's only in that time that we can see one another, because we see out of ourselves through our cracks and into others through theirs. When did we see each other face-to-face? Not until you saw into my cracks and I saw into yours. Before that, we were just looking at ideas of each other, like looking at your window shade but never seeing inside. But once the vessel cracks, the light can get in. The light can get out.

John Green, *Paper Towns*

Creating Shamanic Community

As stated earlier, shamanism is universal. The practices and principles are as available to you and me as they are to the indigenous cultures of any country. But don't be mistaken—there are differences.

Seekers in the Western world do not grow up with the same teachings and values as those in indigenous cultures, so Western seekers have to begin at square one, like infants of an indigenous shamanic culture, learning everything from the obvious to the very subtle about the foundations and philosophies of working together in harmony with others and honoring life, nature, and spirit. This learning is natural, and yet can sometimes be difficult.

Many modern seekers are learning and practicing on their own, and for some, it can feel like a lonely journey. In these cases, it is important for the apprentice to break the Western habit of acting as an island. We are never alone. The helping spirits are always with us, and we must do our part to keep the channels of connection open and flowing. Connecting with nature is one way to keep those channels open. Journeying often is another, and communing with other seekers is yet another. In most cases, Westerners don't communicate with others about their spiritual journey out of fear of rejection or criticism. So they continue to learn and practice alone, not realizing there is a drumming circle just down the road whose members are also learning and practicing in quiet safety.

Being a shaman or practicing shamanism is a personal and individualized experience, but the heart of shamanism is oneness, community, and connectedness.

Being a shaman or practicing shamanism is a personal and individualized experience, but that doesn't mean that you do it all alone, or that you don't need community. On the contrary, the heart of shamanism is oneness, community, and connectedness. As mentioned in the last chapter, connection with others is a very necessary part of human health and well-being. Creating a community that lovingly and honestly supports your choice to live shamanically will serve you well. It can give you the opportunity to observe and learn from others, to ask your friends and family to share their points of view and to be mirrors for you, and to share discoveries and lessons. Being part of a group dedicated to such things as talking, reading books, having discussions, spending time in nature, mirroring for one another, soul healing, drumming, rattling, dancing, singing, journeying, conducting ceremony and ritual, doing community service, and sharing experiences is, in and of itself, a very healing thing.

Individually or with a friend or group, you may enjoy, feel drawn to, and experience great benefits from giving back to the world. One of my shamanic teachers, Dr. Larry Peters, has been studying and practicing Tibetan shamanism for almost fifty years. One day, he shared with me that Tibetan shamans believe that when a person has a problem, that person should do something to help someone else. The teaching is simple yet profound: when we step outside of ourselves and become less self-focused and less attached to our own lives, thoughts, viewpoints, opinions, and feelings, we expand, open up, become compassionate, and begin to intuitively see what is happening for other people and in the world. When we help another person, in whatever way we can, we in turn help ourselves see the bigger picture and our own lives and issues become more clear. When we step outside of our "separate" life, with open eyes, we see the beauty, feel the pain, and find that we really are all one tribe, and always have been.

Mayan priestess Nana Vimla Eufemia Cholac Chicol exemplifies this calling to help others whenever she can. In Figure 31, she is honoring the children at the Prayer Vigil for the Earth in Washington, D.C., in the late 1990s.

Finding and Working with a Shaman, Shamanic Practitioner, Shamanic Teacher, or Shamanic Group

This is an exciting time, ripe with opportunity. The revival of shamanism and the resurgence of the desire to heal, grow, shift, and make a substantive difference in the world are powerful forces causing resources, healers, and teachers to come out of the woodwork, the deserts, and the jungles. They now step forth and offer humanity a healing, guiding hand. Multitudes of people and groups in the United States and all around the world are sharing information about what shamanism is; what shamanic experiences are and feel like; how to enter the nonordinary worlds of spirit; how to connect and build relationships with helping spirits; how to be aware of, garner, and utilize the energies of nature and the nonordinary worlds; and how to heal, be a healer, and shift the realities—essentially, how to practice shamanism.

But with many people being called to share and the many opportunities for you to learn, it may be difficult to discern who to contact or where to go for your healing or training.

One good way to choose the right healer or teacher for you is to ask your local metaphysical, spiritual, or New Age bookstore proprietor and staff who they know, what they know about these people, and who and what they recommend. Wellness, alternative, and complementary healing centers are also good sources. In some communities, the local health-food store is the center of all the action. The occasional physician is also aware of shamanism and practitioners. All of these places and people can be good ways to find out about local practitioners, as well as indigenous traditional shamans. Many stores, healing centers, and some doctors' offices are the hubs of spiritual know-how, and even if they haven't explored shamanism themselves, they will likely know of people who have and are currently doing so.

Figure 31

Exploring the Internet is also recommended. Visit the websites listed in the resources section at the back of this book, or go to *Google. com* and enter *shamanism, shamans, shamanic practitioners, shamanic healers,* or *shamanic teachers* in the search line. These sites will likely contain pages of information about shamanism; the person or group hosting the site; their calling, trainings, philosophies, and services; and perhaps endorsements. Reading this information is a potential first step to finding a shaman, practitioner, teacher, or group. Discernment is the second step. It is important to check within yourself and seek spirit guidance about whether or not this offering is right for you. Follow your intuition. If you feel drawn to a particular way, culture, philosophy, group, or person, check it out. It may be just what you need.

Every shaman, shamanic practitioner, shamanic teacher, and shamanic group is unique, and all have differing practices, philosophies, and specialties.

Every shaman, shamanic practitioner, shamanic teacher, and shamanic group is unique, and all have differing practices, philosophies, and specialties. Likewise, each person seeking shamanic healing or training is unique and has individualized needs and goals. If you are seeking shamanic healing, guidance, or teachings, it is important to find the right fit. It would serve you well to carefully assess your own needs and to take some time to investigate and interview a prospective healer or teacher prior to scheduling a session or attending training. Usually a phone call or a few email exchanges are all that is needed to get a feel for the person and his or her services and philosophies, and to begin to establish a connection.

There are no regulatory, licensing, or accrediting boards or associations for shamanism, and there likely won't be, due to the nature of shamanism and its uniquely individualized practitioners and practices. How can one regulate or license the sharing of gifts from spirit? Yet there are shamanic schools that claim to certify shamans, and there are shamanic practitioners who claim to be certified. This certification may indicate that a shaman or practitioner has reached a certain level of training, experience, and competence, or it may not. It is always best to rely on recommendations, word-of-mouth referrals, endorsements, and your own intuition, gut feelings, truth-spot sensations, guidance, and personal interactions with the healer(s) or teacher(s) that you are considering.

When considering whether a healer, teacher, or group is right for you, look for those who:

- Honor the spirit that moves in all things
- Have a strong, respectful relationship with their helping spirits
- Respect nature and the environment
- Have a powerful healing energy
- Are accepting, nonjudgmental, easy to talk with, fully present with you, and sincerely interested in and focused on what you have to say
- Ask questions
- Are flexible, open, and genuinely caring
- Are honest and speak to the point
- Are well versed in helping people
- Are thoughtful and compassionate, yet not overly coddling
- Are able to effectively help you heal and learn
- Are able to effectively address your healing issues with real, practical methodologies, in partnership with you
- Are available to you in times of need, within appropriate boundaries and reason
- Are recommended or have a reputable standing in the community
- Are not afraid of emotions—yours or their own
- Model integrity, impeccability, and gratitude
- Are always learning themselves (shamans are forever observers and students of life)
- Are inclusive and welcoming
- Have a global view of oneness and the interconnectedness of all things

Avoid those who:

- Tell you what to think or how to act
- Say, insinuate, or imply that their way is the only way
- Reject or make fun of you for giving your opinion, saying things they don't agree with, questioning perceived inconsistencies, or asking questions
- Use belittling words, actions, or attitudes
- Have an arrogant, superior, know-it-all, "I'm better than others," or "I'll tell you" attitude
- Seem to be practicing shamanism just for the money, fame, or power
- Are exclusionary
- Are controlling
- Appear angry, unstable, moody, insensitive, or overly serious
- Are not practical
- Try to be or say they are perfect or *the* expert, or believe and tell you they are enlightened and above the human experience
- Are shortsighted
- Are offensive, crass, or disrespectful
- Ask you to spend a lot of money at any time, especially up front
- Ask for, or appear to be asking for, sexual favors or emotional alliances

If you are considering participating in a shamanic healing or training session, I recommend that you:

- Honor the spirit that moves in all things
- Be open to communication from your own soul and helping spirits

- Be open to the healing, training, energies, and new ideas
- Release the need to be in control without losing the connection with your own intuition, insights, knowings, discernment, wits, and senses
- Release judgment and expectations
- Talk with the healer or teacher, if possible, to see if this healing or training is a good fit for you and to ask any questions you might have
- Spend some time considering what your intentions are and what you would like to get out of and accomplish from the healing or training
- Be prepared to participate and be actively involved in your healing and learning
- Relax and be yourself
- Ask questions and share openly; if this is a group setting, be aware of others and your interactions with the group, and listen to what others share. There is a lot you can learn from other participants.

I recommend that you not attend the session or group if you:

- Don't honor the spirit that moves in all things. If the healer or teacher is integral, and you are playing games or testing your skepticism, he or she may be offended and will let you know, especially if your skepticism disrupts the energy flow, learning, or cohesiveness of a group situation.
- Think you already know it all and are going to assist the healer/teacher
- Are using drugs or alcohol, especially in excess within twenty-four hours of the session
- Are afraid of the healer or teacher. Healers and teachers are people with real-life pains, struggles, and experiences. Real healers and teachers have been there, understand, and can help empower you, if you let them.

The Hollow Bone

Conclusion

The Future Is Yours

We shall not cease from exploration
And the end of all our exploring
Will be to arrive where we started
And know the place for the first time.

T.S. Eliot

"Where do I go from here?" you might be asking at this point. You have some basic information about shamanism, the shamanic way of living, who shamans and shamanic practitioners are, and what they might look like and do. You understand a bit about the initiations that they go through, have a feel for what a calling is, and perhaps are experiencing some recognition and compulsion to move forward in your own calling. If so, you now know some steps to finding shamans, shamanic practitioners, healers, teachers, or groups to investigate further.

The next step is up to you. Does all this information fall into the category of "That's interesting," or the category of "I am compelled to explore this in more depth"?

As you ponder, consider the following thoughts. The first comes from Grandmother Flordemayo. A Mayan shaman and a member of

Figure 32

the International Council of Thirteen Ingenious Grandmothers, she is pictured on the right in Figure 32.

> The sacred Mayan prophecies have stated: a time will come when the eagle of the north shall meet with the condor of the south. At this time, all the tribes will join together and form a Gathering of Elders. In these gatherings, the elders will share their traditions and medicines with each other. When the elders have gathered, they will then disperse to share this ancient knowledge and wisdom with all of humanity. This prophecy has come to pass. I don't consider myself a traditional person, but a universal person. Instead of abiding by rigid rules, I want to be free in my heart.[23]

Tibetan Grandmother Tsering Dolma Gyaltong, also pictured in Figure 32, believes competition and self-importance are the reasons most people don't seek an inner peace.

> "People wish for happiness but do not find it," she said. "A person might, through much suffering, gather a great deal of money during their life . . . but money doesn't bring a person

well-being in the end. The real problem is we do not love each other. We do not have this deep pure love that makes the positive connection. There's not enough of that. If everyone really did a true spiritual practice, which develops into a positive mind, the world would not be in the dire situation we find it in today."[24]

Finally, I leave you with a popular, if loose, translation of a message from the Hopi elders. It is poignant and beautiful, and my Hopi friend assures me that it is accurate; it is something the elders would have said, even if they couldn't put it in these specific English words. (The Hopi and English languages differ, and every translation is just a bit different.)

You have been telling the people that this is the Eleventh Hour.

Now you must go back and tell the people that this is The Hour.

Here are the things that must be considered:

Where are you living?

What are you doing?

What are your relationships?

Are you in right relation?

Where is your water?

Know our garden.

It is time to speak your Truth.

Create your community.

Be good to each other.

And do not look outside yourself for the leader.

This could be a good time!

There is a river flowing now very fast.

It is so great and swift that there are those who will be afraid.

They will try to hold on to the shore.

They will feel like they are being torn apart, and they will suffer greatly.

Know the river has its destination.

The elders say we must let go of the shore, push off toward the middle of the river, keep our eyes open, and our heads above the water.

See who is there with you and celebrate.

At this time in history, we are to take nothing personally, least of all ourselves!

For the moment we do, our spiritual growth and journey comes to a halt.

The time of the lonely wolf is over. Gather yourselves!

Banish the word struggle from your attitude and vocabulary.

All that we do now must be done in a sacred manner and in celebration.

We are the ones we have been waiting for.[25]

You are today where your thoughts have brought you; you will be tomorrow where your thoughts take you. —James Lane Allen

Resources for Personal Healing, Learning, and Exploration

Books, card decks, distance-learning options, DVDs, and CDs for personal learning and healing abound. Good ways to choose the right tool(s) for you are similar to those for choosing the right shaman, shamanic practitioner, healer, teacher, or group. Ask around at your local bookstores, health-food stores, healing centers, and alternative-friendly medical establishments. Find out what they know about and what they recommend. Some folks are quite knowledgeable about shamanism, while others are not.

Websites

Exploring the bountiful Internet is yet another recommendation for learning more about shamanism. Reading the information and the endorsements on the sites you discover is a good way to discern if someone's offering is right for you. Follow your intuition. If you feel drawn to a particular person or organization's website, check it out. The person or group may be just what you need.

There are thousands of websites available on and about shamans, shamanic practitioners, and shamanism. They're hosted by researchers, anthropologists, shamans, shamanic practitioners, shamanic teachers, foundations, societies, organizations, groups, and others offering information, guidance, healings, teachings, and ceremonies. The websites listed here are recommended because they are inclusive—that is, they welcome and post the information of many shamans, shamanic practitioners, and groups from multitudes of cultures, trainings, philosophies, understandings, ways of working, and ways of living. As always, the choice is yours.

Shamanic Teachers and Practitioners
www.shamanicteachers.com

The Shaman's Portal
www.shamanportal.org

The Society for Shamanic Practitioners
www.shamansociety.org

Shaman Links
www.shamanlinks.net

Foundation for Shamanic Studies
www.shamanism.org

Shared Journeys
www.sharedjourneys.org

Tibetan Shamanism
www.tibetanshaman.com

Prayer Vigil for the Earth
www.oneprayer.org

Shamanism Canada
www.shamanismcanada.com

Ice Wisdom
www.icewisdom.com

Riverdrum
www.riverdrum.com

Down to Earth: The Shaman's Circle
www.shamanscircle.com

Link TV, The Power of "WE"
www.linktv.org/globalspirit/wisdom

Transformational Projects
www.dreamchange.org

Shared Wisdom
www.sharedwisdom.com

Other sites about or hosted by shamans mentioned in this book are:

Barb Barton, singer/songwriter
www.barbbarton.com

First Voices Indigenous Radio
www.firstvoicesindigenousradio.org

Gretchen Crilly McKay, shamanic practitioner and teacher, American Sangoma
www.ancestralwisdom.com

Shilo Satran
www.shamansdream.org and *www.sacredtoolmaker.com*

Dee Slate, shamanic practitioner, teacher, and acupuncturist
www.heartfirehealingjourneys.com
www.chesapeakeacupuncturecenter.com

YouTube Postings

There are so many postings to view and more coming on YouTube *(www.youtube.com)* every day. This listing will quickly prove to be a meager sampling of priceless gems. Keep checking; there is a wealth of information coming in rapidly.

Grandma Agnes Baker-Pilgrim: The Natural Way - i-WE Project - Natural Way: Indigenous Voices
www.youtube.com/watch?v=tCto1mhz_f0

First Nations Inc. Buffalo Messengers
www.youtube.com/watch?v=O6db6pkFB1E&feature=player_embedded#!

Gabriel of Urantia Talks with Russell Means
www.youtube.com/watch?v=ORnELir9QCc&feature=related

Diet of Souls—HoustonNorthGallery
www.youtube.com/watch?v=obH96eyIJXs

Ojibwa Grandmother Recounts Walk Around the Great Lakes
www.youtube.com/watch?v=wPega7E8Lhg

Steven Seagal Tells Off BP British Petroleum
After Gulf of Mexico Oil Spill
The need to care for the earth is central to shamanism.
www.youtube.com/watch?v=xpH6ivzcgJk&feature=related

The Spirituality of the Timbisha Shoshone People
www.youtube.com/watch?v=Xk6jGjVXXKc

Indigenous Native American Prophecy
(Elders Speak, part 1 of 6)
All parts are recommended and can be accessed from this one.
www.youtube.com/watch?v=g7cylfQtkDg&feature=related

Tuva: Shamans and Spirits presented by
The Foundation for Shamanic Studies
*www.youtube.com/watch?v=nFmpWmghLB4&feature=player_
embedded*

Notes

1. Sandra Ingerman and Hank Wesselman, *Awakening to the Spirit World: The Shamanic Path of Direct Revelation* (Boulder, CO: Sounds True, 2010), 1.

2. Michael Harner, *The Way of the Shaman*, 3rd ed. (New York: Harper San Francisco/HarperCollins, 1990), 20.

3. Chief Seattle, as translated and quoted by Dr. Henry A. Smith in the *Seattle Sunday Star* on October 29, 1887. Smith's version is reproduced in a 1993 online article by Nancy Zussy, state librarian, Washington State Library, which is available on the website The Nomadic Spirit (*www.synaptic.bc.ca/ejournal/wslibrry.htm*). As Zussy notes, no transcription or translation of Chief Seattle's speech is on record. Smith put together his 1887 version from notes taken at the time.

4. Harner, 69.

5. Ingerman and Wesselman, 16.

6. Tom Cowan, *Pocket Guide to Shamanism* (Freedom, CA: The Crossing Press, 1997), 9.

7. Jeremy Narby and Francis Huxley, *Shamans Through Time: 500 Years of the Path to Knowledge* (New York: Jeremy P. Tarcher/Putnam, 2001), 4.

8. Mihály Hoppál, "Shamanism: An Archaic and/or Recent System of Beliefs," in Shirley Nicholson (ed.), *Shamanism* (Wheaton, IL: Quest Books, 1987), 76.

9. José Stevens, in Ingerman and Wesselman, 11–13.

10. Shilo Satran, personal communication with Colleen Deatsman.

11. Thomas Soloway Pinkson, PhD, "Comprehending Shamanism," web page text on Pinkson's website Nierica (*www.nierica.com*).

12. Richard Noll and Kun Shi, "Chuonnasuan (Meng Jin Fu): The Last Shaman of the Oroqen of Northeast China," *Journal of Korean Religions* 6 (2004), 135–162. Available at *www.desales.edu/assets/desales/SocScience/Oroqen_shaman_FSSForumAug07.pdf*. Accessed February 27, 2011.

13. Agnes Baker-Pilgrim, (Grandma Aggie), "Joining Prayers," *World Pulse* 2 (2005), 37. Available online at *www.worldpulse.com/magazine/editions/global_healing* or *www.agnesbakerpilgrim.org/Page.asp?PID=89*. Accessed February 27, 2011.

14. Wolf story, author unknown. From Colleen Deatsman. *Seeing in the Dark: Claim Your Own Shamanic Power Now and in the Coming Age.* (San Francisco: Red Wheel Weiser, 2009), 223.

15. Joseph Campbell. *Western Quest: Volume 1: Origins of Occidental Mythology* (Minneapolis: Highbridge Audio, 1999).

16. "Jesse Lee Monongye." Comments from a 1998 conversation with the owner(s) of Sedonawolf, an online retailer of Native American jewelry and art. Available at *www.sedonawolf.com/monongye/jesse.html.* Accessed March 1, 2011.

17. Roger Highfield. "Surfer Dude Stuns Physicists with Theory of Everything." *The Telegraph* (November 14, 2007). Available at *www.telegraph.co.uk/earth/main.jhtml ?view=DETAILS&grid=&xml=/earth/2007/11/14/scisurf114.xml.* Accessed March 2, 2011.

18. Neale Donald Walsch. *Friendship with God: An Uncommon Dialogue* (New York: Berkeley Trade, 2002).

19. Miguel Ruiz. *The Four Agreements* (San Rafael, CA: Amber-Allen Publishing, 2000), 1–2.

20. Thomas Banyacya Sr.'s speeches at the Prayer Vigil for the Earth and United Nations, text and translation from Thomas Banyacya Jr.

21. "Angaangaq Angakkorsuaq." Biography on the shaman's website, Ice Wisdom. Available at *www.icewisdom.com/angaangaq.* Accessed March 3, 2011.

22. John Perkins, *Shapeshifting: Techniques for Global and Personal Transformation.* (Rochester, VT: Destiny Books, 1997).

23. Dee Slate, personal communication. Deatsman, 10.

24. John Perkins. *The World Is As You Dream It: Teachings from the Amazon and Andes.* (Rochester, VT: Destiny Books, 1994).

25. Quote available on the website Welcome to the Native Village *(www.nativevillage.org),* under "The International Council of Thirteen Indigenous Grandmothers: Quotes by Grandmother Flordemayo." Available at *www.nativevillage.org/INTERNATIONAL %20COUNCIL%20OF%2013%20INDIGENOUS%20GR/Each%20GR%20 Home%20Page/Tsering%20Dolma%20Gyalthong/1 Tsering%20Dolma%20Gyalthong.htm.*

Bibliography

Andrews, Ted. *Animal Speak: The Spiritual and Magical Powers of Creatures Great and Small.* St. Paul, MN: Llewellyn, 1993.

Bailey-Lessirard, Michele. "Michele Pick Up the Rattle." Article in the author's online journal, *The New Moon Journal.* June 23, 2009. Available at *www.newmoonjournal.blogs.com/the_new_moon_journal/2009/06/pick-up-the-rattle.html.* Accessed March 2, 2011.

Baker-Pilgrim, Grandma Agnes. "The Natural Way - i-WE Project - Natural Way: Indigenous Voices." Video on YouTube. Available at *www.youtube.com/watch?v=tCto1mhz_f0.* Accessed March 2, 2011.

Brown, Joseph Epes. *The Sacred Pipe: Black Elk's Account of the Seven Rites of the Oglala Sioux.* Norman: University of Oklahoma Press, 1989 (originally published in 1953).

Deatsman, Colleen. *Inner Power: Six Techniques for Increased Energy and Self-Healing.* St. Paul: Llewellyn Publications, 2005.

———. *Journey to Wholeness: Personal Healing through Spirit and Soul-Self Connection.* N.p.: 2005. Available in manuscript form from *www.colleen-deatsman.com.*

———. *Seeing in the Dark: Claim Your Own Shamanic Power Now and in the Coming Age.* San Francisco: Red Wheel/Weiser, 2009.

Eliade, Mircea. *Shamanism: Archaic Techniques of Ecstasy.* New York: Pantheon Books, 1964.

Halifax, Joan. *Shamanic Voices: A Survey of Visionary Narratives.* New York: E. P. Dutton, 1979.

Høst, Annette. "The Staff and the Song: Using the Old Nordic Seidr in Modern Shamanism." Article on the website Scandinavian Center for Shamanic Studies. Available at *www.shamanism.dk/Artikel%20-%20 THE%20STAFF%20AND%20THE%20SONG.htm.* Accessed February 28, 2011.

Ingerman. Sandra. *Shamanic Meditations: Guided Journeys for Insight, Vision, and Healing.* Boulder, CO: Sounds True, 2010.

Ingerman, Sandra and Wesselman, Hank. *Awakening to the Spirit World: The Shamanic Path of Direct Revelation.* Boulder, CO: Sounds True, 2010.

Kazlev, M. Alan. "The World Tree." Web page on Kheper, a website with information about various metaphysical topics. Available at *www.kheper. net/integral/tree.html.* Accessed February 28, 2011.

Liberatore, Marcia A. "A Five-Element Analysis of the Grail Myth." *Medical Acupuncture: A Journal by Physicians for Physicians* 17, no. 3 (May 2006). Available at *www.medicalacupuncture.org/aama_marf/journal/vol17_3/article_6. html.* Accessed February 28, 2011.

Louv, Richard. *Last Child in the Woods.* Updated and expanded edition. Chapel Hill, NC: Algonquin Books, 2008.

"Message from the Hopi Elders." Text available for download from the website Community Weaving. Available at *www.communityweaving.org/hopielder.pdf.* Accessed March 2, 2011.

Moss, Nan and Corbin, David. *Weather Shamanism: Harmonizing Our Connection with the Elements.* Rochester, VT: Bear & Company, 2008.

Narby, Jeremy and Huxley, Francis. *Shamans Through Time: 500 Years on the Path to Knowledge.* New York: Jeremy P. Tarcher/Putman, 2001.

Neihardt, John G. *Black Elk Speaks: Being the Life Story of a Holy Man of the Oglala Sioux.* Lincoln: University of Nebraska Press, 1988 (originally published by Morrow in 1932).

Perkins, John. *Shapeshifting: Techniques for Global and Personal Transformation.* Rochester, VT: Destiny Books, 1997.

———. *The World Is As You Dream It: Teachings from the Amazon and Andes.* Rochester, VT: Destiny Books, 1994.

Pinkson, Thomas Soloway. "Comprehending Shamanism," web page text on Pinkson's website Nierica *(www.nierica.com).* Accessed February 27, 2011.

Ruka, Mac Wirema Korako (Macki) and Jim Yellow Horseman. "Prophesies of the Indigenous People of New Zealand." Transcription of an April

1997 interview with Ruka and Yellow Horseman on Manataka, the website of the American Indian Council. Available at *www.manataka.org/page225.html*. Accessed February 28, 2011.

Sanchez, Victor. *Presentation at the Conference on Shamanism*. Santa Fe: The Message Company, 2006.

Stavish, Mark. *The Path of Alchemy: Energetic Healing and the World of Natural Magic*. St. Paul: Llewellyn, 2006.

Teters, Charlene, and Mai, Uyen. "Culture Infused," an art exhibit presenting works of Hopi artist David Dalasohya Jr., California State Polytechnic University, Pomona, November 8–30, 2005. Available at *polycentric.csupomona.edu/news_stories/2005/11/new-la-bounty-chair-of-interdisciplinary-applied-knowledge-presents-culture-infused-art-exhibit.html*. Accessed May 15, 2009.

Thao, Paja. "The Shaman" and "Becoming a Shaman." In "I Am a Shaman: A Hmong Life Story with Ethnographic Commentary." Dwight Conquergood. Minneapolis: Southeast Asian Refugee Occasional Papers, Number Eight, 1989. Available online at *library.thinkquest.org/trio/TTQ04097/*. Accessed February 25, 2011.

Wilber, Ken. "The Deconstruction of the World Trade Center—A Date That Will Live in a Sliding Chain of Signifiers: Part III: The Spiritual Waves Respond." Excerpt from the novel *Boomeritis*. Posted on the website Ken Wilber Online, October 17, 2001. Available at *wilber.shambhala.com/html/books/boomeritis/wtc/part3.cfm/*. Accessed February 28, 2011.

Permissions and Credits for Illustrations

Figure 1: Newspaper Rock Petroglyphs and Pictographs. Photo by Colleen Deatsman (*www.colleendeatsman.com*).

Figure 2: Haru and Univu from Amazonia Brazil. Photo and information courtesy of the website Ice Wisdom (*www.icewisdom.com*).

Figure 3: *Fire Keepers.* Artwork and photo courtesy of Brian Corbiere, Bibamikowi Studios.

Figure 4: Puja dish. Photo by Colleen Deatsman. Information courtesy of Dr. Larry Peters (*www.tibetanshaman.com*).

Figure 5: *Spirit Speaks 3.* Photo by Joy Markgraf.

Figure 6: *Spirit Speaks 2.* Photo by Joy Markgraf.

Figure 7: Medicine Wheel. Art courtesy of artist Adam Kane and Sacred Circle New Age Center (*www.sacredcirclenewage.com*).

Figure 8: Big Horn Medicine Wheel. Photo courtesy of Tim and Candy Strain.

Figure 9: The International Council of Thirteen Indigenous Grandmothers. Photo by Marisol Villanueva, courtesy of the International Council of Thirteen Indigenous Grandmothers.

Figure 10: Martha Lucier and don Marco Nuñez Zamolloa. Photo and information courtesy of Shamanism Canada (*www.shamanismcanada.com*) and photographer Todd Lucier.

Figure 11: Thomas Banyacya Sr. Photo and information courtesy of Thomas Banyacya Jr., photographer Bill Sanda, and Prayer Vigil for the Earth (*www.oneprayer.org*).

Figure 12: Urarina shaman. Photo by Bartholomew Dean.

Figure 13: The late Pau Karma Wang Chuk. Photo and information courtesy of Dr. Larry Peters (*www.tibetanshaman.com*).

Figure 14: *Lady's Slipper*. Art and information from Sleeping Bear Press (*www.sleeping-bearpress.com*) and illustrator Gijsbert (Nick) van Frankenhuyzen (*www.hazelridge-farm.com*).

Figure 15: Grandma Aggie. Photo by Marisol Villanueva, courtesy of the International Council of Thirteen Indigenous Grandmothers.

Figure 16: Ecuadorian shamans in ceremony. Photo and information courtesy of Shamanism Canada (*www.shamanismcanada.com*) photographer Todd Lucier, and Daniel Koupermann (*www.ecuadortravelvacations.com*).

Figure 17: *Tree of Life*. Art and photo courtesy of Illyana Balde.

Figure 18: Pau Karma Wangchuk dance. Photo and information courtesy of Dr. Larry Peters (*www.tibetanshaman.com*).

Figure 19: Eagle Drum. Designed, created, and photographed by Joy Markgraf.

Figure 20: Shaman's mirror. Photo by Colleen Deatsman. Information courtesy of Dr. Larry Peters (*www.tibetanshaman.com*).

Figure 21: Sacred feathers. Photo by Colleen Deatsman. Information courtesy of Dr. Larry Peters (*www.tibetanshaman.com*).

Figure 22: Shaman's rattle. Designed, created, and photographed by Joy Markgraf.

Figure 23: Shaman's rattles. Designed, created, and photographed by Joy Markgraf.

Figure 24: Shaman's eye curtain. Designed, created, and photographed by Joy Markgraf.

Figure 25: Sacred dagger. Photo by Colleen Deatsman. Information courtesy of Dr. Larry Peters (*www.tibetanshaman.com*).

Figure 26: Thomas Banyacya Sr. presenting the Hopi Prophecy. Photo and information courtesy of Thomas Banyacya Jr., photographer Bill Sanda, and Prayer Vigil for the Earth (*www.oneprayer.org*).

Figure 27: Angaangaq Angakkorsuaq. Photo and information courtesy of Ice Wisdom (*www.icewisdom.com*).

Figure 28: *The Legend of Michigan*. Art and information from Sleeping Bear Press (*www.sleepingbearpress.com*) and illustrator Gijsbert (Nick) van Frankenhuyzen (*www.hazelridgefarm.com*).

Figure 29: Dancing Sangomas. Photo and information courtesy of sangoma/shamanic practitioner Gretchen Crilly McKay (*www.ancestralwisdom.com*).

Figure 30: Aama Bombo (Mother Shaman). Photo by Marisol Villanueva, courtesy of the International Council of Thirteen Indigenous Grandmothers.

Figure 31: Nana Vimla Eufemia Cholac Chicol. Photo and information courtesy of photographer Bill Sanda and Prayer Vigil for the Earth (*www.oneprayer.org*).

Figure 32: Tibetan Grandmother Tsering Dolma Gyaltong and Mayan Grandmother Flordemayo. Photo and information courtesy of the International Council of Thirteen Indigenous Grandmothers, photographer Bill Sanda, and Prayer Vigil for the Earth (*www.oneprayer.org*).

The Hollow Bone

About the Author

Patrick Kelley

Colleen Deatsman has been exploring health and wellness, self-healing, personal growth, and spiritual development for over 25 years. She is a Licensed Professional Counselor, Licensed Social Worker, Usui Reiki Master, Certified Clinical Hypnotherapist, Certified Alternative Healing Consultant, Shamanic Practitioner, and the author of three previous books, including *Seeing in the Dark: Claim Your Own Shamanic Power Now and in the Coming Age*. Colleen lives in Mason, Michigan. For information about her trainings and workshops or her online classes in shamanism, visit www.colleendeatsman.com.

To Our Readers

Weiser Books, an imprint of Red Wheel/Weiser, publishes books across the entire spectrum of occult, esoteric, speculative, and New Age subjects. Our mission is to publish quality books that will make a difference in people's lives without advocating any one particular path or field of study. We value the integrity, originality, and depth of knowledge of our authors.

Our readers are our most important resource, and we appreciate your input, suggestions, and ideas about what you would like to see published.

Visit our website, *www.redwheelweiser.com,* where you can subscribe to our newsletters and learn about our upcoming books, exclusive offers, and free downloads.

You can also contact us at *info@redwheelweiser.com* or at

Red Wheel/Weiser, LLC
665 Third Street, Suite 400
San Francisco, CA 94107